The Pe...
[...]
Eas... ...man
...U Coast and
Country Walks

published by
pocket mountains ltd
The Old Church, Annanside,
Moffat DG10 9HB

ISBN: 978-1-907025-65-5

Text and photography copyright © Keith Fergus 2018

Printed in Poland

Introduction

Think of East Lothian and Midlothian and a low-lying, predominantly rural landscape may well spring to mind, yet the Pentland Hills, just south of Edinburgh, rise to nearly 600m in height and provide some of the finest hillwalking in Scotland with magnificent views from the summits. To the east, the Lammermuir Hills may not have quite the same appeal as their near neighbours but they still offer superb hillwalking options, while North Berwick Law, Traprain Law and the Garleton Hills make up for what they lack in height with a succession of incredible panoramas. Away from the high ground are lovely pockets of woodland, wildlife-rich country parks, fascinating historic sites and 65km of coastline between Musselburgh and Dunbar, with some of the best dune-backed beaches in the country.

History

Coal mining, paper making, farming and the manufacture of gunpowder were the industries that fuelled the growth of many of the area's towns and villages, including Gorebridge, Newtongrange, Roslin, Musselburgh and East Linton. Proximity to the Firth of Forth meant fishing was also a key industry, aiding the expansion of Musselburgh, Cockenzie, North Berwick and Dunbar. The historic Herring Road ran for 45km through the Lammermuir Hills and was a crucial through-route for fishwives who carried their huge creels of herring from Dunbar to the markets in Lauder in the Borders.

Coal was mined in Midlothian as far back as the 13th century, but it was not until the late 1800s, with the opening of the Lady Victoria Colliery at Newtongrange, that the industry became a main employer. In 1794 Gore Glen was the site of Scotland's first gunpowder mill while Roslin Glen echoed to the sound of its mills and gunpowder production from the early 1800s.

North Esk Reservoir, which sits deep in the Pentland Hills, provided a constant water source for several local paper mills during the 19th and early 20th centuries while the Rivers Tyne and Esk were home to a number of mills processing wool and grain. The Pentland Hills are thought to have been farmed since the Iron Age when the Votadini tribe first ploughed the valleys, and by the 18th century an important drove route carried livestock through the hills to the great trysts at Falkirk and beyond.

The Romans arrived in Scotland around 80AD and established a fort near the mouth of the River Esk at Musselburgh, while the castles at Tantallon, Dirleton and Dunbar played their part in the frequent fighting between Scotland and England which shaped our nation and identity.

Like much of Scotland, tourism today plays a significant role. Visitor attractions such as the Scottish Seabird Centre at North Berwick, Preston Mill on the outskirts of East Linton and the National Mining Museum of Scotland in

Newtongrange are all hugely popular. East Lothian's glorious coastline, the Pentland Hills Regional Park and several country parks offer plenty for the outdoor enthusiast, with walking, cycling and wildlife watching all bringing people to this corner of Scotland.

The natural environment

Both Traprain Law and North Berwick Law were formed through volcanic activity more than 300 million years ago, with their shapely profiles left behind when the landscape was scoured during the last ice age. Today their summits are great vantage points over much of southern Scotland.

The history of the Pentland Hills goes even further back, with the rocks within the range forming some 420 million years ago. The Pentland Fault pushed parts of the landscape upwards before ice rounded the tops and meltwater eroded the glens. Although not the highest hills in Scotland (Scald Law, the loftiest point in the Pentlands, rises to 579m above sea level), this area offers wonderful walking, scenery and wildlife. Away from the high ground, ancient woodland, riverbanks, open countryside and one of the most celebrated coastlines in the country highlight the diversity throughout the region. Even in towns such as Dalkeith or Newtongrange peace and quiet and far-reaching views are never far away.

No matter where you walk in Midlothian and East Lothian, be it wood or moor,

riverbank or reservoir, farm or village, this is a landscape brimming with wildlife and flowers. Buzzard, kestrel, cormorant, goldeneye, green woodpecker, great-crested grebes, skylark, redshank, plover, roe deer, cinnabar moth and small copper butterfly, harebell, wood sorrel, wood anemone, tormentil and common spotted orchid are a few examples of species that may be seen during the year.

How to use this guide

The 40 walks within this guidebook are between 2km and 14km in length and almost all can be completed within half a day. The region has excellent public transport links and the majority of the walks are accessible by bus or train. Public transport information may have changed from the time of writing and should be checked before commencing any of the walks (travelinescotland.com).

Many of the routes are low level and take advantage of the excellent network of paths. A few walks are child friendly and any rocky, boggy or steep terrain is detailed. It is not advisable to stray from the described routes onto farmland or near exposed cliffs, and where livestock is present dogs must be kept on leads.

A number of the walks cross steep hill or mountain terrain where good map-reading and navigational skills will be needed in poor weather. Winter walking brings distinct challenges with limited daylight hours – and walkers should be aware of strong winds, especially along the coast and over higher ground at any time of year.

Preparation for a walk should begin well before you set out, and your choice of route should reflect your fitness, the conditions underfoot and the regional weather forecasts; www.mwis.org.uk provides daily, accurate forecasts for the Pentland and Lammermuir Hills.

Even in summer, warm, waterproof clothing is advisable and footwear that is comfortable and supportive with good grips is a must. Don't underestimate how much food and water you need and remember to take any medication required, including reserves in case of illness or delay. Do not rely on receiving a mobile phone signal when out walking, particularly away from built-up areas, and many walkers also carry a whistle, first aid kit and survival bag.

Each route begins with an introduction detailing the terrain walked, the start and finish point, the distance covered, the average time to walk the route and the relevant Ordnance Survey (OS) map. None of the hill or moorland walks should be attempted without the relevant OS map and a compass. It is a good idea to leave a route description with a friend or relative in case an emergency arises.

Use of Global Positioning System (GPS) devices has become more common, but while GPS can help pinpoint your location on the map in zero visibility, it cannot tell you where to go next and, like a mobile phone, should not be relied upon.

Until the Land Reform (Scotland) Act was introduced in 2003, the 'right to roam' in Scotland was a result of continued negotiation between government bodies, interest groups and landowners. In many respects, the Act simply reinforces the strong tradition of public access to the countryside of Scotland for recreational purposes. However, a key difference is that under the Act the right of access depends on whether it is exercised responsibly.

Landowners also have an obligation not to unreasonably prevent or deter those seeking access. The responsibilities of the public and land managers are set out in the Scottish Outdoor Access Code (www.outdooraccess-scotland.com).

Sheep, lambs and cattle are found on the Pentland and Lammermuir Hills, as well as lower-lying farmland, throughout the year. During lambing season – March to May – dogs should be kept on a lead at all times on the hills or in areas where livestock graze. The East Lothian coast also provides a rich habitat for many ground-nesting birds, and from April to August dogs should be kept under strict control.

Grouse shooting takes place on the hills between August and December and partridge shooting from September to February; look out for temporary signage with information on where it is safe to access the hills during that day's shoot.

The Pentland Hills rise on the outskirts of Edinburgh and dominate the landscape of the Lothians. Set within the Pentland Hills Regional Park, this rolling range of peaks offers superb walking as the routes in this selection, which extend from its northern boundary, perfectly illustrate. Here, you'll find a real sense of space and remoteness just a few miles from Scotland's capital city.

The windswept summits of Caerketton and Allermuir Hill are among the most cherished by outdoors lovers and offer incredible panoramas that extend to the bigger more muscular mountains of the Southern Highlands. An ascent of Castlelaw, near the centre of the regional park, also comes with magnificent views.

Away from the hills – and just as beloved of walkers – are the reservoirs, which feature in fine lower-level routes where the scenery is as impressive as on the higher ground. The shores of Bonaly, Harlaw and Threipmuir Reservoirs are fringed by excellent paths and tracks which also serve as access points into the very heart of the Pentlands – Scald Law, the highest point of the range, Glencorse Reservoir and beyond.

Around the reservoirs, in the passes and on the tops, there is a vast array of wildlife for the keen-eyed to spot, and buzzard, kestrel, cormorant, goldeneye, heron, tufted duck, swans and migrating geese are among the many birds that can be seen through the seasons as you explore this very accessible range of hills.

The Pentland Hills: North

Caerketton, Allermuir Hill and Capelaw

Distance 9.75km **Time** 3 hours 30
Terrain hill and countryside paths, tracks
and pavement; some steep ups and
downs **Map** OS Explorer 344 **Access** buses
from Edinburgh to Hillend

This magnificent walk takes in the
Pentland Hills' northern peaks of
Caerketton, Allermuir Hill and Capelaw,
with breathtaking views throughout and
a return through open countryside and
the picture-postcard village of Swanston.
Inevitably, such pleasures come at a cost
– here in the shape of a thigh-busting
450m of ascent.

From the Hillend Country Park Car Park
take the left-hand path that shadows the
Midlothian Ski Centre access road, then
climb a steep flight of steps through
woods (waymarked for Caerketton) all the

way to a junction. Turn left and then right
to continue the steep ascent across open
hill. When the path splits go left to reach
a vantage point (with well-placed bench)
over Arthur's Seat and Edinburgh Castle.

Now on a gradual rise, keep right at a
fork, with the path soon reaching a gate at
the base of Caerketton. Beyond this, keep
straight on and tackle the very steep
climb, to the right of a fence – with views
unfolding across the Firth of Forth to Fife.

Brace yourself as you gain 100m of
height in a distance of less than 500m, but
thankfully the gradient now eases for a
gentle pull west past a large cairn before
an easy final stroll onto Caerketton's 478m
summit. Your reward here is a stunning
outlook across Edinburgh and out to Scald
Law while your next objective, Allermuir
Hill, rises sharply to the west.

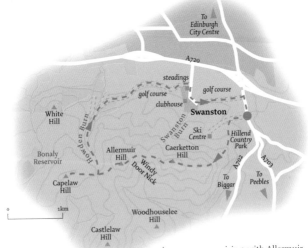

Still keeping right of the fence, the path drops steeply to an airy col, aptly known as Windy Door Nick, at the base of Allermuir Hill, after which a straightforward but unforgiving ascent gets you onto Allermuir's top – at 493m, the highest point on the route. The Ochil Hills are visible to the northwest while, on a clear day, Ben Lomond emerges at the edge of the Southern Highlands.

From the summit go through a gate, then keep right at a fork and descend steeply to a track that runs through Howden Glen. Go straight across this onto a path, climb over a stile and take the right of two tracks to ascend steadily west onto the rounded top of Capelaw.

The summit is not pronounced and can be easy to miss in poor visibility, but it is identified by a large metal post. Again the views are mesmerising, with Allermuir Hill, in particular, beckoning you back.

Retrace your steps as far as the Howden Glen track, then turn left and carry on until you reach a stone outhouse. Take the track on the right here, cross the narrow Howden Burn and continue northeast through a gate and then past a pocket of woodland. Keep right as the path bears east, in the shadow of Allermuir Hill and Caerketton, all the way to a gate.

Beyond this, walk along a single-track road to Swanston Steadings and follow the road left, then right around a courtyard to reach the junction with Swanston Road. Follow this up to Swanston village before bearing left to find a fenced track which crosses the golf course. The track returns you to the A702 where a right turn leads back to Hillend Car Park.

◀ Castlelaw from Allermuir Hill

Over Caerketton

Distance 6.25km Time 2 hours 30
Terrain hill and countryside paths and
tracks; some steep ascents and descents
Map OS Explorer 344
Access buses from Edinburgh to Hillend

Rising steeply just a few miles south of
Edinburgh city centre, the shapely peak
of Caerketton provides one of the finest
views in the Pentland Hills Regional Park
and, what's more, a clear path climbs
all the way to the summit. Rather than
being forced to retrace your steps, you
can enjoy a delightful descent through
the quieter surrounds of Boghall Glen.

From the Hillend Country Park Car Park
take the left-hand path that shadows the
Midlothian Ski Centre access road, then
climb a steep flight of steps through
woodland (waymarked for Caerketton) all
the way to a junction. Turn left and then
right to continue the steep ascent across
open hillside. Where the path forks, keep

left to reach a bench with a view that
extends to North Berwick Law.

Now on a gentle incline, keep right at a
fork, with the path soon reaching a gate at
the base of Caerketton. Beyond this, carry
straight on along a well-worn path to the
right of a fence, with views emerging
across the capital and the Firth of Forth to
the Kingdom of Fife as you climb more
than 100m in a little under 500m.

A gradual pull west takes you past a large
cairn, after which an easy climb gains the
478m summit of Caerketton – which
translates from Brittonic as 'Fort of the
Refuge'. Scald Law, Castlelaw and Allermuir
Hill are just some of the Pentland peaks on
show, while on a clear day Ben Lomond
rears its head in the distance.

Still keeping right of the fence, the path
drops steeply to a bealach between
Caerketton and Allermuir Hill, known as
Windy Door Nick. Cross the fence via a
stile and descend south along a path

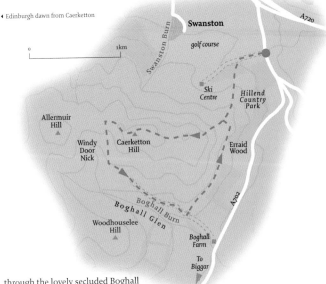

◄ Edinburgh dawn from Caerketton

Swanston

golf course

Swanston Burn

A720

A702

Ski Centre

Hillend Country Park

Allermuir Hill

Windy Door Nick

Caerketton Hill

Erraid Wood

Boghall Burn

Boghall Glen

Woodhouselee Hill

Boghall Farm

To Biggar

0   1km

through the lovely secluded Boghall Glen – keep an eye out for buzzard and kestrel. Beyond another stile, continue beneath the southern slopes of Caerketton all the way to a gate.

Once through this, the path briefly fades and the route can be a little muddy for a short while as it bears southeast across a field. Approaching another gate, pick up a track which continues beyond the gate and past a couple of radio masts. As you near Boghall Farm, leave the track to nip down a waymarked path on the left into a pocket of woodland.

After a few paces, just before a gate, turn left for Hillend and Swanston, keeping left of a fence along the edge of a field. The path wanders through the gorse, a mass

of vibrant coconut-scented yellow in late spring, climbing again past the radio masts. Beyond these, pop through a gap in the fence, then cross a stile. From here another path continues easily through the gorse above the A702, skirting the broadleaf Erraid Wood, a Scottish Wildlife Trust reserve which is home to a fantastic selection of birds, including spotted flycatcher, yellowhammer and treecreeper.

The path eventually reaches a gate; beyond this go left, following the signpost for Swanston. Now a steep ascent leads back to the gate at the base of Caerketton. From here retrace the outward route to Hillend.

Capital view from Swanston

Distance 4km **Time** 1 hour 30
Terrain hill and countryside paths, tracks;
some steep ascents **Map** OS Explorer 344
Access buses from Edinburgh to Hillend

Nestled at the base of the Pentland Hills,
the picturesque thatched cottages of
Swanston village seem a world away from
nearby Edinburgh. This route traverses
the lower slopes of Caerketton to visit the
tranquil community where a young
Robert Louis Stevenson once spent his
summer holidays. Although short, the
walk involves 200m of ascent – but the
inspirational views are ample pay-off.

From the Hillend Country Park Car Park,
take the left-hand path that shadows the
Midlothian Ski Centre access road to reach

a steep flight of steps, signposted for
Caerketton. Climb the steps through
woodland all the way to a junction, here
turning left and then right to continue the
steep ascent across open hillside. When
the path forks, go left to reach a bench
where you can muse on the cityscape laid
out before you, with many of the same
landmarks that would have so inspired
Robert Louis Stevenson in his youth –
Edinburgh Castle, Arthur's Seat and
Salisbury Crags in the west, out to the
Lomond Hills above Fife and eastwards to
the twin landmarks of Bass Rock and
North Berwick Law in East Lothian.

After a gradual ascent, you come to a fork
where you go right and continue until the
path reaches a fence at the base of

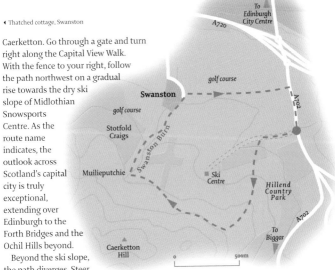

◀ Thatched cottage, Swanston

Caerketton. Go through a gate and turn right along the Capital View Walk. With the fence to your right, follow the path northwest on a gradual rise towards the dry ski slope of Midlothian Snowsports Centre. As the route name indicates, the outlook across Scotland's capital city is truly exceptional, extending over Edinburgh to the Forth Bridges and the Ochil Hills beyond.

Beyond the ski slope, the path diverges. Steer right onto the path that sweeps downhill to gain a track. Keep left here for Swanston and continue under the slopes of Caerketton to another fork. Take the right branch (again for Swanston) and descend gradually northeast above the Swanston Burn, with spectacular views of the Edinburgh skyline. Beyond a gate, bear right onto a firm track and descend through lovely countryside, keeping right at a fork to meet a junction at Swanston.

It is thought that Swanston dates back to the early 13th century when a community grew around a farm leased to a farmer named Sveinn (*Sveinn's Tun* was eventually anglicised to Swanston). Here, you'll find the only thatched cottages left in the city, dating from the 17th or 18th century, while the stone cottages were built for farm workers in the 1850s. There was once a school here, which closed in 1931, while the novelist Robert Louis Stevenson spent his summers here during the late 1800s.

To complete the walk, keep right (or go left if you want to explore Swanston) and follow a fenced track across the golf course for easy progress through scenic countryside, eventually dropping down past Swanston Clubhouse to the A702. Go right and follow the pavement to the start.

Castlelaw

Distance 8km Time 3 hours
Terrain hill paths and tracks; some steep
ascents Map OS Explorer 344
Access buses from Edinburgh and
Colinton to Dreghorn, leaving a short
walk to the start

This exhilarating walk climbs to 488m
above sea level with more than 350m of
ascent as it cuts through the Pentland
Hills Regional Park. Be aware, however,
that Castlelaw also lies within Ministry
of Defence Land where red flags (or, by
night, red lamps) will indicate when live
firing is taking place. Take care not to
wander into areas marked on the OS map
as danger zones at such times.

The start point is a parking area that
sits on a minor road beside the A720
just south of Dreghorn. From Dreghorn,
follow Dreghorn Link as it sweeps right

onto a slip road that heads towards
the A720. After another 13om, before
reaching the dual carriageway, turn
left and follow the minor road to reach
the start point.

From here go through the right-hand
of three gates beside a 'Castlelaw via
the Howden Glen' sign. A wide track
passes through another gate before
continuing southwest in full view of
Caerketton, Allermuir Hill and Capelaw
Hill, across open farmland where livestock
graze. The track, which can be muddy
at points, rises gradually before dropping
down over a burn to continue across
the field.

Continue beyond a pocket of woodland
and then a gate, crossing the Howden
Burn to gain a junction beside an old
stone outhouse. Turn left onto a stony
track signposted for Castlelaw. A steady

◄ Allermuir and Caerketton from Castlelaw

climb south now begins, with few navigational issues, threading through the scenic confines of Howden Glen where skylark, meadow pipit and lapwing are regular visitors.

Soon the track steepens, providing a tough pull, but if a breather is required there are fine views north across Edinburgh. In a while the gradient relents as the route passes a waymarked path on the left that rises onto Allermuir Hill. The view to the southern Pentland Hills, including Turnhouse Hill, is sensational.

The domed summit of Castlelaw now comes into view and, after crossing a stile beside a cattle grid, a short steady climb curls around the shoulder of Fala Knowe from where the track undulates gently to a track on the right. Take this for a steady ascent southwest and then south onto Castlelaw, its broad summit plateau an ideal spot for a break.

Here, you can bask in the fine views – particularly along Glencorse to Scald Law, Carnethy Hill and the shapely top of West Kip, extending beyond Allermuir Hill and Caerketton across Midlothian and East Lothian. To the south sits Castlelaw

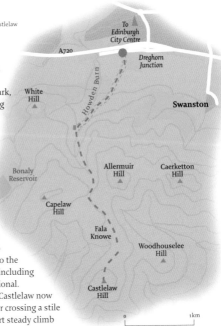

Hill Fort and Earth House which date from around 500BC; it is thought that people lived and farmed here for a 700-year period. The best way to visit is from Castlelaw Farm, signposted off the A702.

The return involves retracing your steps through Howden Glen, enjoying the views across Edinburgh and the Firth of Forth to Fife on this easier downhill ramble.

Bonaly to Capelaw

Distance 6.75km **Time** 2 hours 30
Terrain hill and countryside paths and
tracks **Map** OS Explorer 344
Access no public transport to the start;
buses from Edinburgh to Bonaly, leaving
around 1.25km to Bonaly Upper Car Park

On the northern fringes of the Pentlands,
Bonaly Country Park offers a great
introduction to the area. This route
sweeps through the heart of the country
park to skim the stony shore of Bonaly
Reservoir before escaping to the heights
of Capelaw Hill and returning via scenic
Howden Glen, an historic passage
through the hills. Despite the absence of
any sharp climbs, there is still around
300m of ascent overall.

Cross Bonaly Upper Car Park, go through
a gate and then take the middle track at a
three-way junction for Glencorse. This rises
through woodland all the way to another
gate, beyond which the track continues to
climb south across moorland above the
attractive Dean Burn Gorge, where you'll
find a rolling stock of flora through the
seasons – from winter juniper berries and
cones to spring primroses and summertime
dog violet and pale butterwort. Swift and
skylark flit above the moorland in warmer
months, and there are fine views across
Edinburgh at any time.

The gradient soon eases and, after
passing through another gate, the track
reaches Bonaly Reservoir, surrounded by
woods and a stony beach that makes a
pleasant spot for a break. The reservoir
dates to 1853 and was one of several built to
supply fresh drinking water to the

residents of Edinburgh, but it no longer forms part of Edinburgh's water supply.

After passing the reservoir, go through a gate, then turn left onto a path signed for Allermuir and follow this beneath the western slopes of Capelaw. After 200m, keep right at a fork and begin the ascent towards this peak.

Where the path splits, just before the gradient steepens, keep right and climb to a track. Go right onto this to reach a vague crossroads. Turn right for a gradual ascent on a grassy path that leads SSW for around 400m to a large metal post on the broad summit plateau of Capelaw, with stunning views over Scald Law, Allermuir Hill and Arthur's Seat.

A track descends east, dropping to a stile beside a gate. Hop over this and climb a path to meet a track, beneath the slopes of Allermuir Hill. Turn left along this (for Dreghorn) and descend into the peaceful Howden Glen, enjoying fine views of Edinburgh along the way. After 1.25km the track splits beside an old stone outhouse.

Take the left branch for Bonaly into glorious mixed woodland and wander down through a gate to then skirt to the right of a field. Turn left at a junction to continue west along a field-edge track and cross a large stile. The track takes you straight across a path for Laverockdale. After passing through two gates at the end of the field, a firm path rises steadily, then more steeply up steps into woodland.

Where a path comes in from the left, follow it right and descend to a fork. Keep right and right again at the next junction, cross a footbridge over the Dean Burn and walk back to Bonaly Upper Car Park.

◄ Howden Glen

Harlaw and Threipmuir round

Distance 9.25km **Time** 2 hours 30
Terrain countryside and woodland paths
and tracks **Map** OS Explorer 344
Access no public transport to the start

Good paths and tracks link the reservoirs
of Harlaw and Threipmuir, which boast
scenery and wildlife in equal measure and,
with a chance to dip into the ranger centre
and Edinburgh's only raised bog (best in
summer for its dragonflies), it is a
perennial favourite with families. Walking
boots or wellies should top the kit list –
the return path that skirts the lower slopes
of Black Hill can be very muddy.

Begin from Harlaw Car Park, which is
3km southeast of Balerno. From here,
follow a path signposted for Harlaw
Ranger Centre through woodland, then
cross a minor road. Go through a gate to
reach the ranger centre, which is open daily
and provides plenty of insight into the
surrounding landscape.

Just after the centre, turn right onto a
track for Threipmuir Reservoir and follow
this along the western bank of Harlaw
Reservoir. Both were built in the 1840s for
the Edinburgh Water Company to help
power the mills along the Water of Leith.
Today cormorant, goldeneye and tufted
duck are among the many winged visitors
that thrive on these still waters.

Once across a bridge, the track veers left
to skirt the woodland that fringes Harlaw
all the way to its end. Now follow the track
right to trace Threipmuir's northern edge,
soon coming to a gate. Follow a brief
diversion here before returning to the track
to aim for Threipmuir Car Park.

Just before the car park a path darts left,
signed for Glencorse, threading through a
pocket of woodland to reach a minor road
opposite the Red Moss of Balerno Wildlife
Reserve which is lined with silver birch and
Scots pine and is home to common toad,
cuckoo and hare.

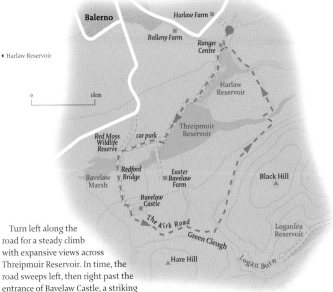

◄ Harlaw Reservoir

Turn left along the road for a steady climb with expansive views across Threipmuir Reservoir. In time, the road sweeps left, then right past the entrance of Bavelaw Castle, a striking towerhouse thought to date from the 17th-century. Keep straight on along a track until just after a gate you join the ancient Kirk Road trail, signed for Glencorse.

This makes its pilgrimage across a field to enter the narrow confines of the Green Cleugh. After almost 1.5km, cross a stile by a gate, then turn left to part company with the Kirk Road. A narrow, well-worn path rises steeply northeast, contouring the lower slopes of Black Hill.

Upon gaining another path, go left for an easy climb. Once over a stile, a boggier section of path descends gently, eventually crossing another stile above Threipmuir.

Walk over a bridge, then go right along an often muddy path beside the reservoir.

The path soon curves left through a gate with a steady ascent now taking you northwest into woodland with fantastic views east towards Bell's Hill and Harbour Hill as you gain height.

At the top, the path passes through two gates before dropping down through more woodland, eventually emerging at a track beyond a gate. Follow this left for just 75m, then turn right onto another track which leads down to a wall beside the wooded eastern banks of Harlaw Reservoir.

Go over a stile here (signposted Harlaw Ranger Centre), turn right and cross a footbridge over a burn. Keeping roughly parallel to the reservoir, a path leads back to the ranger centre near the start.

The Four Reservoirs ramble

Distance 14km **Time** 3 hours 30
Terrain countryside and glen paths and
tracks, minor road **Map** OS Explorer 344
Access no public transport to the start

**Although this circuit stays off the high
tops of the Pentland Hills Regional Park, it
covers a lot of ground – weaving through
two of its most scenic passes and skirting
the still waters of four reservoirs.**

The route begins from Harlaw Car Park,
which is 3km southeast of Balerno. Turn
right onto a waymarked track for
Glencorse, which runs east across a field,
with fine views of Harbour Hill and Bell's
Hill as you progress. After 300m, take the
left branch at a fork and carry on along the
field edge. Beyond a gate, follow the path
that leads gently uphill to another gate.

Depending on the season, a delightful
moorland of vibrant or muted heathery
tones awaits, where lapwing, curlew, snipe,

kestrel and merlin may all be spotted. In a
while, the path descends through a
gate and into the secluded Maiden's
Cleugh, which separates Harbour Hill
and Bell's Hill. A well-worn track continues
southeast, with impressive views of
Carnethy Hill and Scald Law, eventually
dropping down to Glencorse Reservoir.

Once through a gate, turn right onto the
minor Glencorse Road and walk alongside
the reservoir against a backdrop of the
rolling Pentland Hills. Beyond this lovely
body of water, the road runs beside the
Logan Burn before climbing steadily to
Loganlea Reservoir where the outlook
extends to the East and West Kips.

At its far end a gate gives access to a track
which passes the Howe, then crosses a
stone bridge over the Logan Burn. Take an
immediate right onto a stony track for
Balerno – this forms part of the ancient
Kirk Road and soon becomes a grassy track,

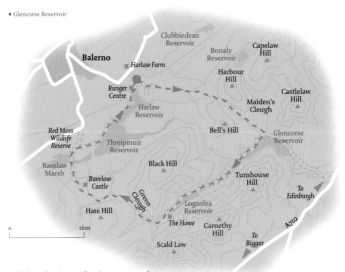

◄ Glencorse Reservoir

which makes its meditative way over the burn and into the sanctuary of the Green Cleugh. After another bridge over the burn, stepping stones soon wander back across it for a final time. A good track then continues through this secluded glen.

Keep left when the track splits and, after crossing a stile, a path leads west out of the pass, eventually crossing a field to meet a gate near the impressive pile of Bavelaw Castle. Beyond the gate, follow a track onto a narrow road. This sweeps left, then right and descends steadily through a cathedral of beech trees before crossing a bridge between Bavelaw Marsh and Threipmuir Reservoir.

After another 250m, beside the Red Moss of Balerno Wildlife Reserve, go right onto a path which weaves through lovely birch woodland. Opposite Threipmuir Car Park, keep right at a fork and continue to a road. This leads back to the waterside, passing the access road for Easter Bavelaw Farm on the far side of Threipmuir Reservoir.

Carry on alongside this reservoir, dog-legging right and then left to continue along the western shore of Harlaw Reservoir. At its end, turn right and cross a bridge to reach Harlaw Ranger Centre. Keep to the road as it turns right to return to Harlaw Car Park at the start.

Green Cleugh to Scald Law

Distance 12km **Time** 4 hours
Terrain hill and glen paths and tracks,
minor road **Map** OS Explorer 344
Access no public transport to the start

Scald Law, the highest point on the
Pentlands range, is usually tackled from
the south side of the regional park, but
this route leaves Threipmuir Reservoir by
the historic Kirk Road and threads
through the Green Cleugh before bagging
the chart-topping peak and its lowlier
neighbours East Kip and West Kip. With
nearly 500m of ascent, the trio make for a
tough but rewarding walk.

Threipmuir Car Park sits 3km south of
Balerno. From the car park's eastern corner,
cross a narrow road onto a path signed for
Glencorse. Pick your way through a patch
of woodland to reach a minor road
opposite the Red Moss of Balerno Wildlife
Reserve. Turn left and continue south

across a bridge between Bavelaw Marsh
and Threipmuir Reservoir, after which the
road rises steadily through an impressive
avenue of beech trees before sweeping
left, then right past the entrance of
Bavelaw Castle.

Carry straight on along a track, then go
through a gate. The ancient path of the
Kirk Road now leads southeast across a
field into the deep defile of the Green
Cleugh, which carves a route between the
slopes of Hare Hill and Black Hill – the
shapely contours of Scald Law dominate
the view ahead. After nearly 1.5km cross a
stile, keep right onto a track and continue
through the pass, shadowing a burn.
Stepping stones breach the burn before it
is crossed twice more via footbridges.

The track now emerges from the Green
Cleugh to reach a lovely old stone bridge
beside the Howe cottage. Don't cross the
bridge; instead go right for a steep

◄ Scald Law from East Kip

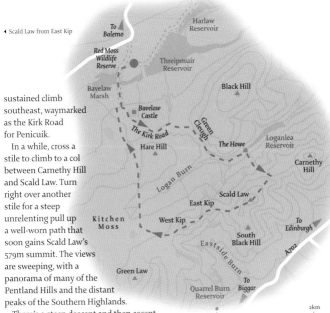

sustained climb southeast, waymarked as the Kirk Road for Penicuik.

In a while, cross a stile to climb to a col between Carnethy Hill and Scald Law. Turn right over another stile for a steep unrelenting pull up a well-worn path that soon gains Scald Law's 579m summit. The views are sweeping, with a panorama of many of the Pentland Hills and the distant peaks of the Southern Highlands.

There's a steep descent and then ascent west to gain East Kip, with a view of Scald Law and the Green Cleugh. The path drops, then rises steeply onto the wonderfully airy ridge of West Kip with its stunning outlook towards the rolling hills of the Scottish Borders.

From West Kip, the path drops steeply to a junction. Turn right for Balerno and follow a clear though sometimes boggy track west and then north across the open moorland habitat of many wild birds, including lapwing and curlew during the summer months. This arena is a fine

vantage point for enjoying unhindered views of the Kips, Scald Law, Carnethy Hill and Turnhouse Hill.

The track continues for nearly 2.5km, with expansive views opening out across the Firth of Forth to Fife. Eventually it drops down to Bavelaw Woods. Go through a gate here, then turn right at a junction onto a single-track road. Follow this for a few paces before diverting left onto the outward route, near Bavelaw Castle. Retrace your steps to the start.

23

This chapter drifts away from the capital to the southern side of the Pentland Hills Regional Park where it eventually nudges the boundary with the Scottish Borders. Here, steep paths lead to the giants of the range in the shape of Scald Law, Carnethy Hill and Turnhouse Hill where the extra exertion is rewarded by some of the best views in Scotland, sweeping across East Lothian, Fife, the Scottish Borders and the Southern Highlands.

Such is the variety of paths that criss-cross the Pentlands – including the old Kirk Road, one of the most historic routes in the country – that the approach routes to the range seem endless, each leading you through a new

landscape which offers up a wholly different perspective on the hills.

The walks that stray from the tops are every bit as varied. Above Glencorse Reservoir sits one of the finest vantage points in the area, while a straightforward route to the lonely Tytler Memorial offers pause for reflection on the lives of the Edinburgh worthies who once owned a swathe of this landscape. An easy loop taking in North Esk Reservoir provides a quiet respite from some of the more trampled routes of the popular peaks.

Back on the high ground and there's a hint of medieval history at Monks Rig on an ascent of West Kip – perhaps the most perfectly formed of all the Pentland Hills.

The Pentland Hills: South

The Tytler Memorial

Distance 3.25km Time 1 hour
Terrain woodland and countryside paths
Map OS Explorer 344 Access bus from
Edinburgh and Dumfries to Boghall

This short route follows good paths
along field edges and through pleasant
woodland to reach a memorial to the
Tytlers, a locally landowning family of
Edinburgh worthies who kept company
with a number of luminaries and literary
greats of the Scottish Enlightenment.

Begin from the small car park at Boghall
Farm which sits on the west side of the
A702, just south of Damhead, on the
eastern edge of the Pentland Hills.

At the car park's western corner go
through two gates, then follow a fenced
path. This goes around the perimeter of
the farm before dropping down into the
attractive wooded Boghall Glen. This is a
lovely little spot, with Boghall Burn
carving a route through the broadleaf

woodland, which is particularly vibrant
during autumn.

Once over a footbridge spanning Boghall
Burn, climb steps through the trees,
ignoring a path to the right and instead
keeping on uphill to a gate. Beyond this,
turn right and follow a field-edge path as it
sweeps left on a gradual ascent to a strip of
beech woodland at the top of the field.

Follow the path as it wanders south
through this sylvan scene with views
across the low-lying Lothian countryside.
In a while it passes through a gate, with
the impressive house at Fulford below to
the left. Continue through the wood and,
beyond another gate, follow the left edge
of a field, brushing past the trees, with the
rounded summit of Castlelaw Hill coming
into view.

After around 200m the path bears left
and drops down over a track. Continue for
a few paces, then cross a stile on the right
and walk down a path through more

◀ The Tytler Memorial

woodland, crossing a footbridge over a burn. The path now rises steadily over a field before picking its way up through a number of rhododendron bushes to a stile.

This gives access to the Tytler Monument which stands in an open area with a commanding view along the East Lothian coastline, all the way to North Berwick Law. The memorial dates from 1893 and is dedicated to James Tytler who owned Woodhouselee Estate during the 18th century. The Celtic red sandstone cross rests on a plinth with a metal plate near its base bearing the Tytler family coat of arms.

Other family members inscribed on the plinth are William Tytler, who was born in 1711, a lawyer and eminent antiquarian writer, and his son, Alexander Fraser Tytler, born in 1747, a Scottish advocate, writer and historian. They are all buried in a family vault in Greyfriars Kirkyard.

From the memorial it is a simple matter of retracing your steps to Boghall, enjoying the surrounding countryside as you make your descent.

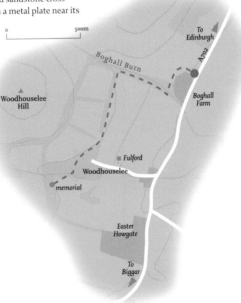

Glencorse Reservoir

Distance 4.25km **Time** 1 hour 30
Terrain minor road, countryside and
riverside paths **Map** OS Explorer 344
Access no public transport to the start;
bus from Edinburgh and Dumfries to the
Flotterstone road end, leaving 250m to
the start

You needn't climb the highest Pentland
peaks to revel in some of the finest
scenery the Pentland Hills Regional Park
has to offer – the paths and tracks above
Glencorse Reservoir deliver sumptuous
views for relatively little effort. On return,
the route meanders alongside Glencorse
Burn and the now disused filter beds.

From Flotterstone Ranger Centre, where
there is ample free parking, take the
woodland path that runs west, parallel to
the Glencorse access road. Turn right and
carry on when it joins the road, keeping an
eye out for traffic.

Carry on past a gate on the left,
signposted for Scald Law (this is the return
route), and climb gently with good views
towards the shapely profile of Turnhouse
Hill. After nearly 1km, turn right from the
road through a gate which is signposted
for Castlelaw.

There's now a steady climb northeast
through gorse – sheep graze on this part of
the route, so keep dogs on leads. The
rounded profile of Castlelaw rises ahead
while the view to the south extends to the
Moorfoot Hills. When you reach the track
beside the Ministry of Defence firing range,
turn left for Glencorse Reservoir.

The route creeps along the edge of the

◄ Glencorse Reservoir

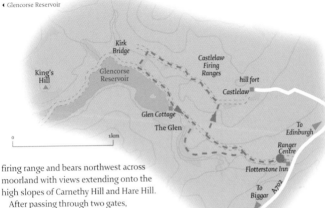

firing range and bears northwest across moorland with views extending onto the high slopes of Carnethy Hill and Hare Hill.

After passing through two gates, Glencorse Reservoir comes into view. Continue along the track to reach a strip of pine woodland and a gate, signed for the reservoir. Before heading down the path it is worth drinking in the view along the water, deep in the heart of the Pentland Hills. The reservoir was constructed in 1822 to help provide Edinburgh with clean drinking water, and today is the focal point of one of the most popular low-level Pentland strolls for its easy access and picturesque setting.

Follow the path as it descends on the right of the wood to a gate. Once through, turn left onto the Glencorse access road and make your way southeast alongside the reservoir, which is flanked by impressive stands of Scots pine. Once past Glencorse Fly Fishery, the road reaches the eastern edge of Glencorse Reservoir.

Go through a gate and pass Glen Cottage; then, after another 300m, leave the road to turn right through a gate for 'Flotterstone by the Old Filter Beds'. An enchanting path drops through woodland to Glencorse Burn and here continues along the riverbank, passing a couple of stone buildings and the site of the old filter bed system. The three beds were installed between 1852 and 1853, and allowed nearly four million gallons of water to be filtered every day.

Continue along the path, soon passing through two gates in quick succession, beyond which a track leads to a gate by the Glencorse access road. Beyond, turn right and retrace your steps to Flotterstone.

Carnethy and Turnhouse Hills

Distance 11.25km **Time** 4 hours
Terrain minor road, countryside and hill
paths **Map** OS Explorer 344 **Access** no
public transport to the start; bus from
Edinburgh and Dumfries to Flotterstone
road end, leaving 250m to the start

Few routes illustrate the diversity of the
Pentlands landscape as clearly as this
ascent through Glencorse and over the
twin peaks of Carnethy and Turnhouse
Hills. Good paths climb to almost 600m
above sea level and, in poor visibility,
navigation and map-reading skills will be
put to the test.

From the Flotterstone Ranger Centre,
where there is ample free parking, follow
the woodland path that runs west, parallel
to the Glencorse access road. When it
emerges onto the road turn right and
continue, keeping an eye out for traffic.

Carry on past a gate on the left,
signposted for Scald Law (which is the
return route), and climb gently along the
road. It soon levels off and passes through
a gate at Glen Cottage where a very
pleasant section of walking wanders along
the northern shore of beautiful Glencorse
Reservoir with the steep slopes of
Turnhouse Hill and Carnethy Hill ahead.
Mallard, whooper swan and great crested
grebe may well be seen out on the water.

Beyond Glencorse Reservoir, the road
shadows the Logan Burn before climbing
steeply to reach Loganlea Reservoir.
Another attractive section of easy walking
continues along the waterside with the
outlook taking in the East and West Kips.

At the head of Loganlea go through a
gate and follow a track past the Howe
cottage, after which you swing left to cross
an old stone bridge spanning the Logan

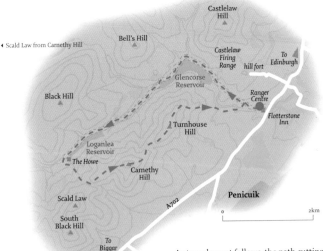

◀ Scald Law from Carnethy Hill

Castlelaw Hill

Bell's Hill

Castlelaw Firing Range

hill fort

To Edinburgh

Glencorse Reservoir

Ranger Centre

Black Hill

Flotterstone Inn

Turnhouse Hill

Loganlea Reservoir

The Howe

Carnethy Hill

Scald Law

A702

Penicuik

South Black Hill

To Biggar

0   2km

Burn. Take the path of the old Kirk Road for Penicuik, pausing to think on the parishioners who tackled this steep climb every week in order to worship at their parish church.

After crossing a stile, the path comes to a col between Carnethy Hill and Scald Law with a spectacular view of the northern Pentland peaks such as Caerketton and Allermuir Hill.

Turn left for a steady pull to the northeast up the western slopes of Carnethy Hill, with Loganlea Reservoir far below. Approaching the top, the gradient steepens a little for a last push to Carnethy Hill's 573m summit cairn, the highest point of the walk with open views across Midlothian, Fife and East Lothian.

A steep descent follows, the path cutting through heather-clad slopes to another col. Continue northeast for another stiff pull past a cairn. Beyond this, a final climb gets you onto Turnhouse Hill's 506m top with a magnificent view over much of the regional park, Traprain Law and the Lammermuir Hills.

Now an excellent track descends north, then northeast across open hillside before tapering to a path that drops steeply. Once through a pocket of woodland, descend to a gate – after which the path continues over an undulating little ridge and down to a convergence of burns and two bridges.

Take the left bridge over the Glencorse Burn to a gate. Turn right beyond this, follow a track through another gate, then turn right onto the Glencorse access road and retrace your steps to the start.

The Kirk Road to Loganlea Reservoir

Distance 7.5km **Time** 3 hours
Terrain minor road, countryside and
hill paths **Map** OS Explorer 344
Access no public transport to the start;
bus from Edinburgh and Dumfries to
Silverburn, leaving 1km to the start

Few journeys to church in centuries past
could have been better suited to godly
contemplation than that of the Kirk Road,
worn down by the feet of faithful
parishioners making their way from
Loganlea and beyond to Penicuik.
Although it avoids the higher peaks this
route tots up an airy 400m of ascent with
heavenly views along the way.

Begin from either of two lay-bys on the
north and south side of the A702, 1km
northeast of the small settlement of
Silverburn. Take care crossing this very fast

and busy road to reach a gate signposted
for Balerno.

Beyond this, join the Kirk Road, an
ancient thoroughfare that extends for
around 5km to Bavelaw above Threipmuir
Reservoir. Historically, this drove route
also provided access for parishioners in
the hill communities of Bavelaw and
Loganlea to make their way to Sunday
worship in Penicuik.

Follow the path northwest over open
farmland (where dogs should be kept
under control), soon crossing the Grain
Burn via stepping stones with Carnethy
Hill and Scald Law rising ahead. After
another 100m, keep left at a fork – ignoring
a waymarked footpath on the right which
is for the return journey – and continue to
tread in the footsteps of the faithful on
the Kirk Road.

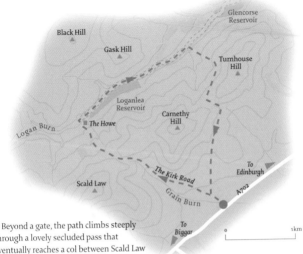

Beyond a gate, the path climbs steeply through a lovely secluded pass that eventually reaches a col between Scald Law and Carnethy Hill. The Kirk Road now descends, with superb views of Hare Hill and Black Hill. Once over a stile, a grassy track drops down into the heart of the Pentlands, reaching a track at the Howe cottage.

Leave the Kirk Road behind by crossing an old stone bridge over the Logan Burn, then turn right onto a track for Flotterstone via Glencorse. After a gate follow the Glencorse access road (watch out for traffic) along the length of Loganlea Reservoir, enjoying good views of Turnhouse Hill and Castlelaw.

Beyond the reservoir the road descends by the fast-flowing Logan Burn and past the entrance drive of Logan House. In another 30m, just before a cattle grid, cross a footbridge over the Logan Burn and go through a gate on the left. An initially boggy track rises towards the col between Carnethy Hill and Turnhouse Hill. As you gain height, the track improves greatly with views opening out across the Pentlands to the Ochil Hills.

The track eventually narrows to a path and runs left of a fence to reach the col. Beyond a gate, turn left onto a path and, after a few paces, keep right at a fork. A narrow sometimes muddy trail bears south, skirting the lower slopes of Carnethy Hill before dropping gradually southwest across open moorland. In a while it rises gently to cross a stile.

A grassy waymarked footpath then descends steadily across a field back to the Kirk Road. Retrace your steps across the Grain Burn to the A702.

◀ Turnhouse Hill

Carnethy Hill, Scald Law and the Kirk Road

Distance 6.5km **Time** 2 hours 30
Terrain minor road, countryside and hill
paths **Map** OS Explorer 344 **Access** no
public transport to the start; bus from
Edinburgh and Dumfries to Silverburn,
leaving 1km to the start

This hill walk crosses the two highest
Pentland peaks before descending the
Kirk Road which historically linked hill
communities with their parish church.
Scald Law and Carnethy Hill are usually
tackled from Flotterstone, but this
delightful alternative follows quiet paths
where the more open landscape makes for
far-reaching views throughout.

Begin from either of two lay-bys on the
north and south side of the A702, 1km
northeast of the small settlement of
Silverburn. Take care crossing this very fast
and busy road to reach a gate signposted
for Balerno.

Beyond this, join the Kirk Road, an
ancient route that extends for around 5km
to Bavelaw, above Threipmuir Reservoir.
Follow the path northwest over open
farmland (where dogs should be kept under
control), soon crossing the Grain Burn via
stepping stones with Carnethy Hill and
Scald Law dominating the view ahead.

After another 100m, keep right at a fork
to leave the Kirk Road for a grassy

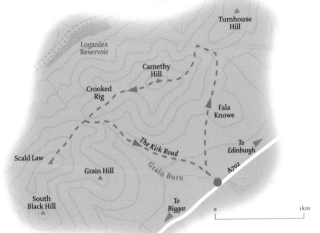

waymarked footpath that leads northeast across a field. This rises steadily, with fine views extending south across Penicuik to the Moorfoot Hills, reaching a stile at a fence. Once over, a boggy path travels across heather moorland towards Carnethy Hill. After 100m keep left when the path splits and continue on a gradual ascent, rounding the lower slopes of Carnethy Hill.

The path soon curves left (northwest), eventually reaching a col between Turnhouse Hill and Carnethy Hill beside a gate. Don't go through the gate, but instead turn left and take the well-worn path that climbs sharply southwest. It is a steep pull but the gradient relents on approach to the large summit cairn.

At 573m Carnethy Hill is only 6m lower than Scald Law, the highest point of the Pentland Hills. The panorama extends across Glencorse to Black Hill and Bell's Hill, all the way to the Firth of Forth and

the Forth Bridges. To the northeast prominent landmarks include Traprain Law, North Berwick Law and Bass Rock.

Scald Law is the next objective, so carry on across Carnethy Hill's summit and take the obvious path descending WSW all the way down to the Kirk Road. Beyond a gate, there's a sustained ascent along a clear path to reach the summit, which stands 579m above sea level.

After enjoying the view sweeping down to the Scottish Borders and out to the Southern Highlands, return to the Kirk Road and turn right to follow the path as it drops steeply southeast through a narrow pass. The landscape soon opens out and a gradual descent takes you to a gate in a wall. Beyond this the Kirk Road crosses open fields to pick up the outward path just north of the Grain Burn. Retrace your steps from here to the start.

◀ West Kip and East Kip from Scald Law

West Kip by the Monks Rig

Distance 7.25km **Time** 2 hours 30
Terrain countryside and hill paths
Map OS Explorer 344 **Access** no public
transport to the start; bus from Edinburgh
and Dumfries to Nine Mile Burn road end,
leaving 200m to the start

There can be no finer introduction to the
joys of the Pentlands than this classic
circular route which climbs along the
scenic Monks Rig, passing the medieval
Font Stone before making a pilgrimage of
West Kip, the most shapely of the
Pentland Hills. The way back is via a
secluded glen with stunning views.

The walk starts from the small car park
beside a row of cottages at Nine Mile
Burn. Facing the cottages, turn left and walk
along the road. Where it turns right, carry
straight on through a gate waymarked for
Balerno by the Monks Rig and Braid Law.

A field-edge path then approaches another
gate, but swings left just before reaching it
to continue on a steep climb.

At the top of the field, cross a stile and
turn right to the next gate, but again
ignore it and stay left to follow the path
that rises along the lower reaches of
Monks Rig – *rig* being the Scots word for
'ridge'. This keeps left of a fence to reach a
stile. Cross this and, after a few paces,
another stile onto the defined Monks Rig.

Climb steeply north, the gradient easing
as the path passes the Font Stone. It is
thought that, rather than being a font, the
deep indentation in the stone held the
base of a cross and may have marked the
route of a pilgrims' path.

An easy incline leads onto the rounded
dome of Cap Law, where the wonderful
outlook includes the Firth of Forth and the
steep slopes of West Kip. Crossing the

◄ East Kip from West Kip

summit, the path splits so keep right and descend north.

Once across a track, continue down over a stile at a sign for Balerno and Monks Rig. From here bear east with a very steep pull quickly gaining the airy summit of West Kip. Its 551m top provides a fine vantage point for the full range of the Pentland Hills as well as many of the muscular Southern Highland mountains.

Retrace your steps to the stile at the base of West Kip. Don't cross it; instead go left along a track for 20m before crossing a stile on the right waymarked for Nine Mile Burn via Braid Law. Once across another track, follow a path which makes a gentle descent south, then southeast beneath Cap Law and above a lovely little glen. After crossing another stile the path widens to a track, after which it curves right to gain a junction above Westside.

Turn right to climb a track to a dip between Braid Law and Cap Law and now carry straight down a path to the Quarrel Burn. Once across this, continue southwest through a secluded glen with stunning views towards the rolling hills above Peebles, eventually reaching a stile a little west of Quarrel Burn Reservoir. Continue, soon crossing another stile.

Make a left turn onto a field-edge path, which then sweeps right and rises, before crossing another stile back onto the outward route. From here retrace your steps to Nine Mile Burn.

North Esk Reservoir

Distance 8.25km **Time** 2 hours
Terrain countryside paths and tracks,
minor road **Map** OS Explorer 344
Access no public transport to the start;
bus from Edinburgh and Dumfries to
Nine Mile Burn road end, leaving 200m
to the start

North Esk Reservoir lies beyond the
boundaries of the Pentland Hills Regional
Park on the fringes of the Scottish
Borders. Built to help power a number of
local paper mills, it is now a fantastic
haven for wildlife. This route approaches
the reservoir by a firm track, then leaves
its lonely shores to return via the
conservation village of Carlops.

The walk starts from the small car park
beside a row of cottages at Nine Mile
Burn. Facing the cottages, turn right and walk
southwest along a narrow road, crossing a

bridge over the Monks Burn. The road rises
gently for nearly 500m to the access road
for Spittal Farm, signed for Buteland by
North Esk Reservoir. Turn right and walk
towards the farm.

Just before you reach the main farm
buildings, swing right onto a public
footpath that climbs steeply and curves
left around the back of the farm. After
crossing a narrow burn, a track rises
steadily west between Patie's Hill and
Spittal Hill with marvellous views
extending south across the Scottish
Borders. The incline eases a little as
progress is made and, after crossing a stile
beside a cattle grid, the track crests at the
440m contour line.

Beyond another stile, a steady descent
begins, with the landscape opening out
over North Esk Reservoir to The Mount
and Wether Law – it is a beautiful setting

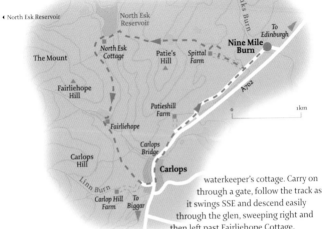

◄ North Esk Reservoir

with a wilder air. The track then drops steeply all the way to a gate; beyond this continue along the southern edge of North Esk Reservoir, a great spot for a break.

Sitting at over 300m above sea level and fed by the Gutterford and Henshaw Burns, the reservoir was completed in 1850 at a cost of £15,093 (this equates to around £900,000 today). It provided a constant watersource for several local paper mills during the 19th and early 20th centuries, including Bank Mill, which produced paper for banknotes. Today it is popular with anglers and a huge diversity of birdlife, including mute swan, redshank, black-headed gulls, tufted duck, cormorant, common sandpiper and oystercatcher.

Beyond the reservoir keep left for Carlops when the track splits, passing the old waterkeeper's cottage. Carry on through a gate, follow the track as it swings SSE and descend easily through the glen, sweeping right and then left past Fairliehope Cottage.

After another 750m the track passes the entrance road of Carlop Hill Farm before emerging beside the A702 at Carlops, an attractive linear village founded in 1784 when the local laird set out a row of cottages on either side of the Edinburgh to Biggar road to house cotton weavers.

Carefully cross the road, turn left and follow the pavement north through Carlops. After crossing a bridge over Fairliehope Burn, pick up a pavement on the north side of the A702, then bear left up steps, waymarked for Nine Mile Burn. A path rises to a minor road, just south of Patieshill Farm. Carry straight on and follow this all the way to a junction, turning left onto another minor road here. This scenic road is easily followed for 1.5km back to Nine Mile Burn.

Many of the towns and villages in Midlothian developed during the Industrial Revolution, and the region once resonated with the sounds of gunpowder mills and coal mines. Clues to this heritage are still visible today, though nature has reclaimed a number of sites.

It is hard to reconcile the gunpowder-rocked past of Gore Glen and Roslin Glen with the havens they have become, where little shatters the peace and the wooded margins are host to a variety of wildlife.

The story of Newtongrange lies in its collieries, particularly Lady Victoria Colliery which today houses the superb National Mining Museum of Scotland. A walk around the village offers a fascinating insight into Midlothian's industrial history.

Enigmatic Rosslyn Chapel transports you much further back in time. Not for nothing did this 15th-century Gothic chapel feature in the 2003 internationally bestselling decoding mystery *The Da Vinci Code* and subsequent Hollywood film adaptation, for very little is as it seems here, and it has attracted droves of tourists (and Grail pilgrims) ever since. Intrigue abounds also at Carberry Hill, with its links to the ill-fated Mary, Queen of Scots and her errant third husband, the Earl of Bothwell.

Roslin Glen, adjacent to Rosslyn Chapel, and almost as popular, is one of three country parks in Midlothian. With more than 1000 acres to lose yourself in, Dalkeith Country Park is also a walkers' playground while the Victorian pile of Vogrie House lies at the heart of the eponymous country park, characterised by sweeping carriage drives, tree-framed views and wildlife-rich woods.

Montagu Bridge in Dalkeith Country Park ▶

Midlothian

Gore Glen

Distance 2km **Time** 45 minutes
Terrain woodland and riverside paths
Map OS Explorer 345 **Access** no public
transport to the start; trains from
Edinburgh and Tweedbank to Gorebridge
or buses from Edinburgh to Gorebridge,
leaving a short walk to the start

Take a short blast through Scotland's
former Gunpowder Glen, where
watermills once powered the production
of this most volatile of materials.
Thankfully today it plays host only to an
explosion of wildflowers in summer
(there are more than 60 species, including
rarities such as broadleaved helleborine
and bird's nest orchid). Come at the right
time and you may also encounter siskin,
dipper, kingfisher, heron and common
blue damselfly in and around the Gore
Water or within the birch and alder trees.

Gore Glen Woodland Park Car Park sits
just off the west side of the A7, 1.5km north
of the B6372 Gorebridge turn-off. There is
room for around 20 cars.

From the car park take the path that
crosses the railway bridge. Once over,
turn right onto another path and follow
this as it runs northwest along the edge
of attractive mixed woodland. It begins
to descend gradually into Gore Glen before
levelling off and continuing through
enchanting wooded countryside.

After 500m look out for a flight of
wooden steps on the left. Go down
these to a small car park beside a minor
road, just before a roadbridge that crosses
the River South Esk. Turn left through
a gate onto a track signposted for
Gorebridge, but leave this immediately
by bearing right onto a path and following
this to the Gore Water. Meander along its
bank to reach an old packhorse bridge.

This is a beautiful spot, the riverbank

◄ Old packhorse bridge in Gore Glen

cloaked in woodland where dipper may well be spotted. Perhaps surprisingly, due to its tranquil nature, Gore Glen was the site of Scotland's first gunpowder mill in 1794 and for nearly 70 years the river was used to drive 10 waterwheels.

Continue along the east bank of the river away from the bridge, soon returning to the track you left when you entered the woodland from the small car park. Turn right onto the track and carry on beside the Gore Water, flanked by the steep wooded slopes of Gore Glen. Go right when the track forks; after passing a waterfall in another 200m or so, the track splits again.

Keep right down steps onto a path that takes you past a wildlife-rich pond, where dragonflies and damselflies may well be spotted during the summer months. Steps then climb left to take you away from the river. After another 30m, go up a steep flight of steps on the left to emerge high above the glen.

At the top turn left onto a path, which shadows the A7 and the railway line. Once through a clearing, where spectacular views extend across Midlothian to the Pentland Hills, the path enters alder woodland. Once back at the railway bridge, cross the tracks and return to the car park.

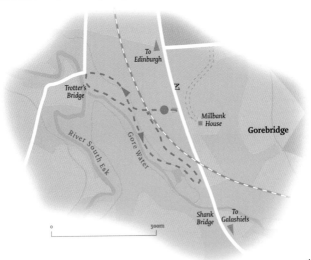

Newtongrange colliery and community

Distance 3.25km **Time** 1 hour
Terrain pavement and parkland paths
Map OS Explorer 345 **Access** trains from
Edinburgh and Tweedbank to
Newtongrange; buses from Edinburgh
and Gorebridge to Newtongrange

The village of Newtongrange, a few
miles southeast of Edinburgh, is
dominated by the iconic brick chimneys of
the excellent National Mining Museum of
Scotland, formerly the Lady Victoria
Colliery. This little walk winds around the
rows of houses built to accommodate
local miners and their families and
provides a fascinating insight into the
Midlothian coal industry.

The route begins from the National
Mining Museum of Scotland, a hugely
popular visitor attraction that tells the story
of 'The Lady', as the colliery was known
locally. The mine was opened in 1895 and

named after Lady Victoria Alexandrina
Montagu Scott, the wife of Schomberg Kerr,
the 9th Marquess of Lothian, who was
chairman of the company between 1890 and
1900. Newtongrange was the ideal location
due to its position above Midlothian's rich
coalfield, as well as its proximity to the
Edinburgh and Hawick Railway Line. Lady
Victoria Colliery closed in 1981, but today a
visit to the museum, which is open daily, is
highly recommended.

Facing the museum turn left and follow
the pavement alongside Murderdean Road
(A7), passing the Lingerwood Cottages that
were built for workers of the Lingerwood
Colliery, which started coal production in
1798. Turn left onto Stobhill Road which
rises gently along the southern edge of
Newtongrange. Upon reaching
Monkswood Road turn left and follow this
quiet street to its end, at a junction beside
Maesterton Place and McLean Walk.

◄ National Mining Museum of Scotland

Keep straight on along a paved path, then a road to a junction. Go left onto Lingerwood Road, then second right onto a road waymarked 'Path Bypass'. After a few metres it sweeps left, but keep straight on along a narrow lane. This runs right of a grid system of tight streets (named First to Tenth Street) lined with old miners' cottages, which offer a glimpse into the community that would have built up during Newtongrange's industrial heyday.

As the lane continues, you have superb views of the Pentland Hills before coming to Seventh Street, the only one of these streets that is signed, after 600m. Turn left, walk to its end, then turn right onto Park Road. After a few paces, go left through a gate into Welfare Park. Keep straight on along a path and, when it splits, bear right and continue to a roundabout. Go straight on to reach a war memorial, then emerge from the park onto Main Street (B703).

Ahead is the Dean Tavern, one of Scotland's few remaining 'Gothenburg' pubs. Originating in Sweden in the late 19th century, 'Goths' were an attempt to regulate and control the consumption of alcohol amongst the working classes. They were not intended to be welcoming or attractive, with no credit, gambling or games (even dominoes!) allowed, and all profits were to be put back into improving the local community. The Dean Tavern was built for the miners and their families who worked at the Lady Victoria, Lingerwood and Bryans Collieries and continues to play a vital role in the local community.

Turn left and follow Main Street through Newtongrange, passing several more attractive, single-storey miners' cottages (some dating from 1872) and a fine statue dedicated to all mine workers. Walk back to Murderdean Road, turn left and return to the start.

45

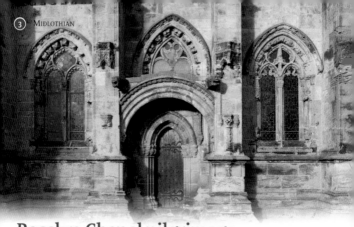

Rosslyn Chapel pilgrimage

Distance 8km **Time** 2 hours
Terrain woodland and countryside paths and tracks, minor roads **Map** OS Explorer 344 **Access** buses from Edinburgh and Penicuik to Roslin

Rosslyn Chapel is one of Scotland's most distinctive buildings and its popularity as a visitor attraction went through the roof after its role in Dan Brown's bestselling 2003 novel *The Da Vinci Code*. Set off in pursuit of your own adventure with just a little decoding required as the well-waymarked route unravels through glorious countryside.

Rosslyn Chapel overlooks the quiet village of Roslin. The chapel was founded in 1446 (although it took some 40 years to complete) by William St Clair for his family and staff and dedicated in 1450 as the Collegiate Chapel of St Matthew. It is still under the ownership of the family more than 570 years later. As well as featuring in

various theories involving Freemasonry, Knights Templar and the Holy Grail, the magnificent interior features intricate stone carvings which depict the Seven Deadly Sins, the Seven Cardinal Virtues, the Dance of Death and various apostles and martyrs. It is open all year round.

Start from the Rosslyn Chapel Car Park on Chapel Loan, just beyond Roslin's Main Street. Before reaching the chapel and visitor centre, turn right onto a narrow road and go down past the graveyard. At the road end, keep straight on (for Roslin Glen Gunpowder Mills) and follow a path high above a steep wooded gorge to emerge onto the B7003.

A few paces along the pavement to the left and a left turn down a long steep flight of steps, signed for Roslin Glen, skips a loop in the B-road, rejoining it further on via a path. Now turn left, cross a bridge over the River North Esk and follow the pavement for 400m before turning right onto a minor

◄ Rosslyn Chapel

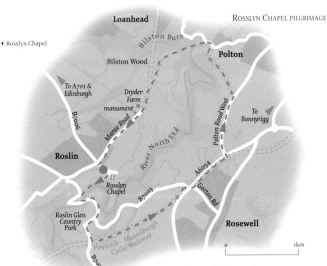

road for the Penicuik to Musselburgh cycle/walkway. The road rises gradually, soon veering left to a waymarked gate on the left, just before a bridge. Beyond this, a path drops to an old railway platform. Here turn right, follow the platform under the bridge and then turn left onto the Penicuik to Musselburgh cycle/walkway which follows the route of the old railway line between Edinburgh and Peebles. The track offers easy walking for 1.5km until it reaches the A6094 near Rosewell where there are great views of the Pentland Hills.

Carefully cross the road, turn left, cross Gorton Road, then continue along the walkway. Go past Hawthornden Cemetery, bear left at a Tyne Esk Trail signpost, cross back over the A6094 and then follow Polton Road West towards

the village of Polton. After 850m turn left onto a lane at Montrose Stables.

Just before the lane ends, bear right and follow a path down to a junction at Polton. Turn left onto Polton Road, cross a bridge over the River North Esk and then continue to a gate on the left, signed for Roslin and Bilston. A narrow path enters more beautiful woodland and rises steeply up steps before continuing high above the Bilston Burn and the River North Esk.

When the path splits keep straight on, waymarked for Roslin, soon picking up a narrow lane. This threads its way through scenic countryside and under an old railway bridge before emerging through a gate onto a single-track road. Pass Dryden Farm and the Mountmarle monument, commemorating the Battle of Roslin in 1303, onto Manse Road. Carry on back to Roslin and turn left for the car park.

Roslin Glen Country Park

Distance 4km **Time** 1 hour 30
Terrain woodland and countryside paths
and tracks, pavement **Map** OS Explorer 344
Access buses from Edinburgh and
Penicuik to Roslin

A wander through Roslin Glen gives more
than a fleeting glimpse into Midlothian's
industrial past and, in particular, its
gunpowder mills which were drawn into
munitions production for battlefields
from the Napoleonic era onwards. This did
not make the glen the safest of environs,
but nowadays the most alarming thing
you are likely to encounter is the rat-a-tat-
tat of a green woodpecker or the cobalt-
blue flash of a kingfisher.

Start from the Rosslyn Chapel Car Park
on Chapel Loan, just beyond Roslin's Main
Street. Before reaching the chapel and
visitor centre, turn right onto a narrow

road and descend past a graveyard. At the
road end, keep straight on (signed for
Roslin Glen Gunpowder Mills) and follow
a path high above a steep wooded gorge.

At the B7003, take a few paces along the
pavement to the left where a left turn down
a long steep flight of steps, signed for
Roslin Glen, provides a handy shortcut,
rejoining the B-road further on via a path.
Turn right onto the pavement and, as it
swings right uphill, carefully cross the road
and enter Roslin Glen Country Park.

A wide track leads through broadleaf
woodland (watch for green woodpecker and
buzzard), soon dropping gently to pass what
was the site of a gunpowder mill from 1803
to 1954. Explosives and gunpowder, used in
the mining and quarrying industries, were
manufactured here. The mills also supplied
munitions for the Napoleonic, Crimea and
the First and Second World Wars.

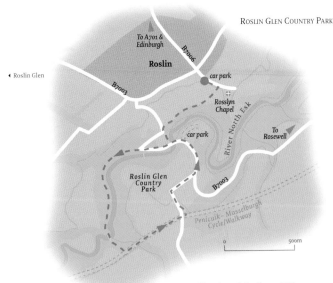

◀ Roslin Glen

After another 200m, go left onto a path and walk down some steps to the River North Esk and the impressive remains of several mills. Hemmed in by the steep gorge, with the river tumbling past, this is a picturesque spot suited to exploration.

It's immediately apparent why this was such an ideal location for the industry that would have resonated through the glen, with the river providing a constant power source, timber and coal readily available and the ports on the Firth of Forth nearby. The valley and trees also helped contain any accidental explosions.

A flight of steps to the left of a stone bridge clambers back to the main track. Turn left, cross a footbridge over the river – home to dipper, kingfisher and even otter – bearing left after a few metres to climb steps all the way to the Penicuik to Musselburgh cycle/walkway. This runs along the old railway line from Edinburgh to Peebles which once linked many of Midlothian's industrial towns and mills.

Turn left and follow the walkway, soon passing under a bridge. After another 100m bear left onto an old railway platform to duck under a roadbridge before turning left, opposite a sign for Roslin Glen Country Park. Make your way up this path to go through a gate beside the bridge, now turning right to walk down the minor road with views to the Pentland Hills as it sweeps right to the B7003.

Carefully cross the road before turning left to follow the pavement downhill. Once past the entrance to Roslin Glen Car Park, cross a bridge over the River North Esk, then turn right onto the outward path and retrace your steps to the start.

Dryden Tower from Roslin

Distance 7.25km **Time** 2 hours
Terrain woodland and countryside
paths and tracks, minor roads
Map OS Explorer 344 **Access** buses from
Edinburgh and Penicuik to Roslin

Most visitors to the village of Roslin have
their sights fixed on the enigma of
Rosslyn Chapel, but it is a shame to miss
the clues to the area's history that lie in
the landmarks scattered around it. This
trail through beech woodland and rolling
countryside sets out to discover a Gothic
folly, a wrought-iron viaduct and a
memorial to one of the bloodiest battles
of the Scottish Wars of Independence.

Begin from Roslin, by the war memorial
at the corner of Penicuik Road and Manse
Road. Follow Manse Road northeast away
from the village centre to its end, after
which the road narrows. Watch out for
traffic on this tree-lined route as it
continues through quiet countryside all
the way to the Battle of Roslin Memorial.

The monument commemorates
an early battle in the Scottish Wars of
Independence when an English army led
by Sir John Segrave was defeated by a
much smaller Scots force on 24 February
1303. Perhaps because the Scots were led by
John Comyn, Guardian of Scotland at the
time, the victory is not as celebrated as
those of his rival, Robert the Bruce, who
would later murder Comyn by the altar in
Dumfries' Greyfriars Church to claim the
crown of Scotland for himself.

Take a path to the left of the memorial,
signposted for Bilston, and follow this
northwest through lovely beech woodland.
Beyond a gate carry on to a three-way fork
and take the centre path, again for Bilston,
continuing above a gorge to a farm track,
which heads towards the B7006.

Just before the road, turn right onto a
path that dives back into the trees, cross a
footbridge and accompany the Kill Burn
(on your right) all the way to a junction.
This watercourse's grim name is thought

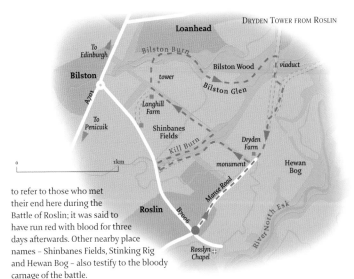

to refer to those who met their end here during the Battle of Roslin; it was said to have run red with blood for three days afterwards. Other nearby place names – Shinbanes Fields, Stinking Rig and Hewan Bog – also testify to the bloody carnage of the battle.

Turn left onto a fenced grassy track and climb gently through the countryside with great views of the Pentland Hills and across Midlothian. Ahead is the striking outline of Dryden Tower.

Once through a gate, just before Langhill Farm, turn right and then left through another gate, after which a path passes near Dryden Tower. Built in the mid-1800s as a hilltop 'eyecatcher', it was part of the policies of Dryden House, which was demolished in 1938 to make way for Bilston Glen Colliery. The tower isn't open to the public and can't be accessed.

Once past Langhill Farm, go through two gates on either side of a track after which another fenced path (waymarked for Loanhead Railway Path) descends gently to a junction. Go right for Bilston Viaduct back into woods, cross a bridge over the

Bilston Burn, then turn right at a junction. After another 150m, bear left up a steep flight of steps to emerge out of the woodland beside a small industrial site.

A wide track continues east, passing two paths on the left. Take the third path, then at a junction keep right. This track, which soon tapers to a path, ends beside Bilston Viaduct. Cross this magnificent structure with its glimpses down into the wooded gorge below. It was built in 1892 by the North British Railway Company and restored in 1999 by Midlothian Council and the Edinburgh Green Belt Trust.

At the viaduct's far end, turn left onto a path signed for Polton which leads to a farm track. Turn right and, once through a gate, follow the road past Dryden Farm to the Roslin Memorial. Retrace your steps to the start from here.

Dryden Tower

Dalkeith woodland wander

Distance 4.25km **Time** 1 hour 30
Terrain woodland and riverside paths
Map OS Explorer 345 **Access** buses from
Edinburgh and Gorebridge to Dalkeith

Dalkeith Country Park is a delight for walkers, with more than 1000 acres of deciduous and pine woodland, riverside and parkland. Owned by the Duke of Buccleuch, it is a working estate but there is a network of paths and walkers are most welcome. This route wends its way through beautiful woods and along the banks of the twin rivers that hold the heart of the park in their embrace.

There is car parking at the Town Gate entrance to Dalkeith Country Park, with a small charge to enter the estate, although children are free. Beyond the ticket kiosk, where the access road splits, go left and carry on past the fabulous Dalkeith Palace, which was built in 1702 and is the former seat of the Duke of Buccleuch. A number of famous people have stayed at Dalkeith Palace, including Bonnie Prince Charlie, who lodged here for two nights during the Jacobite Rebellion of 1745, while King George IV visited in 1822 and Queen Victoria in 1842.

Carry on to a fork, branch left onto a stony track and follow this towards the impressive single-arch Montagu Bridge that spans the River North Esk. Just before the bridge, bear right and walk down a path to reach the banks of the river.

A good trail meanders north through attractive beech woodland, which is a carpet of bluebells and ramsons during May. There's a short steep climb to emerge high above the river before you drop back down to shadow the fast-flowing waters.

After a more gradual ascent, the path reaches a junction where you turn left. Now the path skirts birch and oak woodland with views extending across open countryside – look out for buzzards

◄ Dalkeith Estate woodland

wheeling above. Keep left when the path splits and continue northeast past a number of venerable old oak trees. Beyond a stile, the path dips back down to the River North Esk.

Once past a footbridge on the left, the River South Esk and River North Esk meet. Turn right – two stone pillars are all that remain of a bridge that once spanned the River South Esk – and follow the path upstream above the South Esk as it winds its way through pleasant woodland, much of it carefully managed for centuries.

In a while, the path widens to a track and culminates beside a gate. Don't go through this; instead take the fenced path to its left. This continues high above the river and runs through more woodland to arrive at a junction. Go right to pass above the old stableyard, now home to an excellent café, restaurant and retail spaces.

Upon reaching the access road you can detour to visit the stableyard or go straight across the access route onto a path that rises gently up to a road. To return to the start, turn left on the road, then go right at the next junction and make your way back along the main drive.

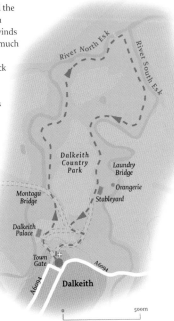

Dalkeith and the Esk explorer

Distance 7.5km **Time** 2 hours
Terrain woodland and countryside paths
and tracks **Map** OS Explorer 345
Access buses from Edinburgh and
Gorebridge to Dalkeith

**Circumnavigate Dalkeith Country Park
on a wider loop that explores the estate's
outlying swathes of scenic countryside and
woodland, as well as visiting the striking
Montagu Bridge and the Orangerie.**

There is car parking at the Town Gate
entrance to Dalkeith Country Park and a
small charge to enter the estate, although
children are free.

Beyond the ticket kiosk, where the access
road forks, go left and carry on past
Dalkeith Palace. Where the road splits,
take the left branch onto a stony track and
follow this over the splendid Montagu
Bridge that spans the River North Esk.

There is a fine view of Dalkeith Palace

from the bridge which was built in 1792 by
Robert Adam as a gift from the Montagu
family to the Buccleuch family to celebrate
the marriage of Lady Elizabeth Montagu
(whom the bridge is named after) and
Henry, 3rd Duke of Buccleuch.

Once across, keep straight on along an
estate road for 300m, then turn right at a
crossroads. Follow a track north through
the estate, keeping an eye out for estate
traffic as well as cyclists. It soon veers a
little to the right and descends gently. Here,
the incongruous sound of traffic on the
A702 City Bypass is a reminder that the
estate is on the edge of Scotland's capital
and the hubbub of city life is never far away.

After climbing a short even slope, keep
left when the track splits, now running to
the left of a wall. The track then curves
right to a junction where you turn left to
dive down to the River Esk and under the
A68 Dalkeith Bypass. Continue away from

◀ Dalkeith Palace

the river with the track now skirting the Castlesteads Park, where roe deer, buzzard and raven may be spotted.

The route veers right and then left past a house before proceeding easily for just over 500m. Here, beside a lovely stone house, the track splits – go right and carry on, enjoying expansive views across Midlothian, all the way to the River Esk, which you cross via the old stone Smeaton Bridge.

From here, a narrow country road rises gently above the river to a T-junction. Turn right and carry on, keeping right when the road diverges. Now follow the road southwest, crossing a bridge over the A68 Bypass.

With meadows fringed by woodland and far-reaching views to the Pentland Hills and Arthur's Seat, a glorious section of the walk now returns to the southern end of Dalkeith Country Park, the road eventually running above the River South Esk.

Cross the Laundry Bridge and follow the estate road past the striking Orangerie, a mock Gothic building dating from the 1840s which was designed by William Burn as a centrepiece to the estate's formal garden. Further on, the old stableyard, now known as Restoration Yard and home to a café, restaurant and retail spaces, is a good place to rest your feet before you return to the car park at the Town Gate via the access road.

Vogrie Country Park

Distance 3.75km **Time** 1 hour
Terrain woodland and riverside paths
Map OS Explorer 345 **Access** no public
transport to the start

The mansion and parkland at Vogrie offer
walkers a slice of the Victorian elegance
that its original owners would have
enjoyed. Situated 4km east of
Newtongrange, it makes a welcome
getaway from the capital with stately
Vogrie House as its centrepiece and a
network of paths radiating out to woods,
landscaped grounds, riverbanks and the
wildlife-rich Tyne Valley Grasslands.

Vogrie Country Park Car Park (pay and
display) sits on the east side of the B6372,
1km south of Dewartown. From here, join a
path waymarked for Vogrie House that
runs to the left of the nursery and a picnic
area. Keep right at the next fork and follow

the same signs to pass a pond and arrive at
the access road beside the country house.

The lands of Vogrie were purchased by
James Dewar in 1719, and his great-
grandson, Lt Colonel Alexander Cumming
Dewar, built Vogrie House in 1876. Since
then the building has also been used for a
time as the Royal Edinburgh Hospital for
Mental and Nervous Disorders, a base for
the Civil Defence Force during the Cold War
and a police headquarters.

Go straight across the access road onto
an area of grassland and follow this to the
right of the house. After crossing a path
that leads from the car park, pick up a trail
waymarked for Tyne Valley and Alderdean.

Follow this into woodland and, at a
crossroads, turn right for Alderdean. Here,
a path rises gently through a glorious mix
of arboreal splendours, including beeches
whose trunks are several metres in

◀ Vogrie House

circumference, and native oak, ash, rowan and alder.

Beyond the beeches, there's a fairly steep descent into a glen to reach a junction. Go right, again for Alderdean, then left to cross an old stone bridge over the Alderdean Burn. In spring and summer, the woodland floor is a carpet of bluebells, wood sorrel, buttercup and primrose, with jay, great spotted woodpecker and nuthatch among the residents you may see or hear.

After a steady climb, the path drops and then swings sharply left. Once over a boardwalk, the path crosses a footbridge spanning the Tyne Water, beyond which it rises through the very different open landscape of the Tyne Valley Grasslands where views unfurl across the country park

and buzzard and sparrowhawk are your most likely overhead companions.

Continue high above the Tyne Water before re-entering woodland and dipping steeply back to the river, passing over this via a footbridge. Now keep left, following signs for Vogrie House, over another foot crossing, this time bridging the Vogrie Burn as it joins the Tyne Water. At the next junction go right to shadow the Vogrie Burn to a stone bridge over it.

Don't cross, but instead go left to follow the signpost for Tyne Valley. Soon after crossing a footbridge, turn right and head up a flight of wooden steps towards Vogrie House. A fairly steep climb takes you back to the crossroads; walk past the house to return to the car park.

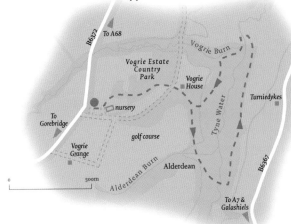

Carberry Hill and Queen Mary's Mount

Distance 2.25km Time 1 hour
Terrain woodland paths and tracks
Map OS Explorer 351 Access no public
transport to the start; bus from Penicuik
and Musselburgh to Carberry, leaving
200m to the start

The attractive woodland of Carberry Hill is owned and managed by the Buccleuch Estate. A series of paths and tracks slip through the wooded lair of birds, roe deer and foxes to the site of a stand-off in which Mary, Queen of Scots surrendered her freedom in exchange for the fair treatment of her third husband, the Earl of Bothwell, who was suspected of murdering her previous husband.

The little village of Carberry lies 3.25km southwest of Musselburgh with Carberry Hill rising to the north of the A6124. Begin from a small car park at the end of the narrow road of Springfield Steading,

nipping round a barrier to follow a track. In just 50m, turn left onto a boggy path for a gradual climb through an ever-changing mixed woodland, where the rat-tat-tat of green woodpecker may keep you company.

Swinging right to a crossroads, you turn left onto a firmer track that continues its easy ascent through the estate to a viewpoint. The vista extends across fields, where you may spot grazing roe deer, to much of the high ground that embraces Edinburgh, including the Pentlands, Arthur's Seat, Blackford Hill, the Braid Hills, Corstorphine Hill and beyond to the Ochils.

After veering right to arrive at another crossroads, go left onto a track that rises gently to a fork. Keep left and then, after a few paces, bear right onto a path coming in from the left. Stay left at the next junction and follow a track to reach the impressive commemorative stone and views out to East Lothian and Fife.

◄ The Pentlands from Carberry Hill

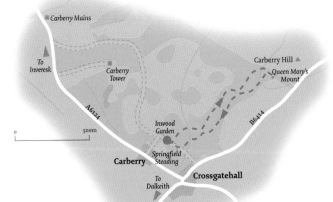

The stone marks the spot where, on 15 June 1567, Mary, Queen of Scots surrendered herself to Protestant Scottish nobles, known as the Confederate Lords, who vehemently opposed the marriage of Mary to the Earl of Bothwell who had been implicated in the murder of Mary's second husband, Lord Darnley.

The Battle of Carberry Hill was more of a stand-off between Mary, Bothwell and their army and the troops of the Confederate Lords, however, and after several hours Mary yielded, apparently persuaded by the Lords' promises of Bothwell's fair treatment. It was the last time she saw Bothwell; he fled Scotland but was captured in Norway and died 10 years later, insane and chained up in a Danish dungeon. Mary was taken to Edinburgh, then imprisoned in Lochleven Castle in Kinross and spent the rest of her life a captive of her cousin Queen

Elizabeth until she was finally tried for treason and executed at Fotheringhay Castle in 1586.

Retrace your steps for 50m to the fork in the track and go left along a path, which skirts the woodland beside a field edge with expansive views beyond the estate across the Midlothian countryside. The path makes its gradual descent through very pleasant scenery, with clumps of primrose and swathes of bluebell on the ground in spring and the possibility of spotting tiny treecreeper darting mouse-like up the trunks.

At a fork, go right and drop back down to the crossroads encountered on the outward route. Turn left onto a track for another easy descent, in time curving right to return once again to the outward route at a crossroads. As before, do not rejoin it; instead keep left to follow a track that sweeps right back to the car park.

The level terrain of the East Lothian hinterland is too often passed over for the drama of the county's stunning coast, but this is to miss out on a mellow agricultural landscape that enjoys some of Scotland's highest levels of sunshine and contains many wonderful low-level and hill walks. The long rolling barrier of the Lammermuir Hills to the south of the county cannot claim the same ease of city access as the Pentlands, but for this reason it enjoys a wilder and more secluded feel.

An endless panorama is the reward for tackling the Garleton Hills above the historic village of Athelstaneford, while the expanse of farmland ironed out beneath the slopes of dinky Traprain Law

makes the views from the summit all the more spectacular.

This diminutive volcanic plug overlooks the village of East Linton where walks to Preston Mill (which featured in the *Outlander* TV drama series) and historic Hailes Castle leave through beautiful countryside, as does the lovely linear stroll between Gifford and Bolton.

The Royal Burgh of Haddington is the geographical hub of East Lothian and its streets and buildings are brimming with history, though the bustle can swiftly be left behind by tracing the banks of the River Tyne. Peace is restored, too, at Pressmennan Wood where a sculpture trail provides fun for all the family.

Near East Linton ▶

Haddington to the Lammermuir Hills

Hailes Castle by the River Tyne

Distance 5.5km **Time** 1 hour 30
Terrain pavement, riverside paths, minor
road **Map** OS Explorer 351 **Access** buses
from Edinburgh and Berwick-upon-Tweed
to East Linton

Associated with Lord Bothwell, infamous
third husband of Mary, Queen of Scots,
Hailes Castle holds a commanding
position above a loop in the River Tyne. Its
crumbling remains are more extensive
than may first appear and can be explored
after shadowing a picturesque section of
the river from East Linton.

Begin from Bridge Street (B1377) beside
the elaborate fountain in East Linton
village centre. Walk down to Station Road
(B1407) and turn right, heading under the
railway bridge before bearing left onto a
private road signposted for Hailes Castle.

After the last house go right onto a path
and continue southwest alongside a
wooded section of the River Tyne, which
rises in the Moorfoot Hills and journeys for
almost 50km to reach the North Sea near
Dunbar. Pass under the A199 and continue;
in a while a steep flight of steps takes you
high above the river with a good view of
Traprain Law before another flight drops
you back to the riverbank. Continue under
the roadbridge that whisks the A1 across
the river, after which the path runs beside a
field and then through more woods – keen
eyes may spot heron, dipper and possibly
even kingfisher along the riverbank.

After 2.5km the path reaches a
footbridge, again waymarked for Hailes
Castle, beside the beautiful cottage of
Hailes Mill. Cross the bridge over the river,
then follow the path uphill to the narrow

Brae Heads Loan (watch out for traffic). A right turn along the road brings you to Hailes Castle which sits on a meander in the river with a commanding view over the surrounding countryside.

Hailes Castle was built by the Gourlay family as a fortified manor house in 1240. Having supported the English during the Wars of Independence, the Gourlays subsequently lost the castle and lands to the Hepburn family. It is thought that James Hepburn, 4th Earl of Bothwell and third husband of Mary, Queen of Scots – who was also implicated in the murder of Mary's second husband, Lord Darnley – may have been born in Hailes Castle. It is open all year.

Retrace your steps along Brae Heads Loan, passing the outward path and continuing northeast on an easy walk with fine views of Traprain Law and the River Tyne. The road runs under the A1 roadbridge and, as it approaches East Linton, passes several houses before swinging left down to the A199.

Carefully cross this busy stretch of road onto Lauder Place. Follow the pavement down under a railway bridge to Station Road. Turn left, cross a lovely stone bridge over the River Tyne, then turn right onto Bridge Street to return to the start.

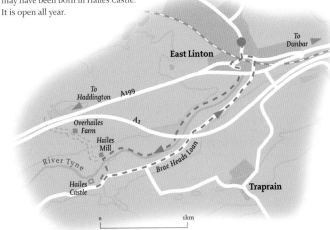

East Linton and Preston Mill

Distance 9.5km **Time** 2 hours 30
Terrain pavement, field paths, minor road
Map OS Explorer 351 **Access** buses from
Edinburgh and Berwick-upon-Tweed to
East Linton

Take the scenic route from East Linton to
the storybook Preston Mill with its
beguiling Dutch-style roof and an equally
delightful architectural oddity, the
Phantassie Doocot, just across the water.
The mill is top of the to-see list for fans of
the *Outlander* TV drama series in which it
featured, and is open through the summer.

East Linton, which sits about 8km east of
Haddington, is a charming village which
developed during the 16th century when
mills were built to harness the power of the
River Tyne. Sited on the outskirts of the
village is Preston Mill which from the 1700s
turned grain into animal feed and meal for
the neighbouring Smeaton Estate. When

operations ceased in 1959 it was the last
working mill in East Lothian. Now in the
hands of the National Trust for Scotland, it
is popular with fans of the historical time
travel TV drama *Outlander*, which first aired
in 2014. Tours present the opportunity to
do some time travel of your own with a
glimpse into the world of those whose
lives revolved around Preston Mill.

From Bridge Street (B1377), beside the
elaborate fountain in East Linton village
centre, walk onto the High Street and out
of the village. After 1km, at Dunpender
Road, cross the B1377, go through a gate
onto the John Muir Way and head uphill.

Beyond a gap in a wall, go left, then right
up wooden steps to climb a path and then
a track to a radio mast with a superb view
of East and West Lomond, North Berwick
Law and Traprain Law. The track now
descends across farmland and, after some
old farm buildings, comes to a junction.

◄ Preston Mill waterwheel

Go straight across this to follow the John Muir Way (here a path) for 850m to a bridge on the left. Cross this and continue into a small pocket of woodland on a track that swings right and then left.

Exiting the wood, the track follows a field edge before keeping right of Kamehill Farm. Go straight on at a crossroads and take the rough farm road all the way to a minor road just right of Stonelaws Farm. Turn right to leave the John Muir Way for a 1km roadside stretch through peaceful countryside (keep an eye out for traffic).

Turn right onto a road signed for East Linton and Binning Wood which gradually southeast with views towards the Lammermuir Hills. In a while the road runs alongside Binning Memorial Wood. Although this was first planted in 1707, much of it was felled during World War II and then replanted about 60 years ago.

Beyond this, the road climbs gently before dropping down to a T-junction. Turn right onto the B1407 and carefully follow the roadside verge, around a couple of blind bends,

towards East Linton. Just before the village the entrance to Preston Mill is on the left.

This beautiful building, distinctive because of its unusual shape and conical red pantile roof, is well worth a visit (open from April to October). Follow the B1407 back into East Linton and the start.

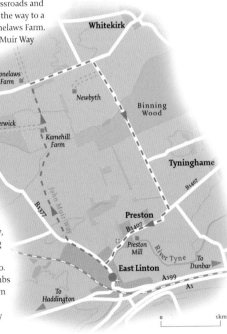

Traprain Law

Distance 2km **Time** 45 minutes
Terrain hill paths **Map** OS Explorer 351
Access no public transport to the start

A stiff climb leads to the summit of Traprain Law, the whaleback hill that rears from the landscape with seemingly endless views despite its lowly stature at only 221m above sea level. With a history of human occupation dating back more than 3000 years, the hill also hid a hoard of Roman silver until it was unearthed just a century ago. Today it is home to a small herd of semi-feral Exmoor ponies.

A small car park sits on the south side of a minor road, at the base of Traprain Law's northern slopes, 4km south of East Linton. From here walk past a couple of picnic benches, then go over a stile to follow a path west, running left of a wall beneath the steep slopes of Traprain Law. Even at this early stage there is a stunning view of North Berwick Law.

After 125m, where the path splits, keep left and climb a boggy well-worn path, which soon steepens with far-reaching views opening out towards Edinburgh, Arthur's Seat and the Pentlands. When the path splits again, go left, then keep right at the next fork before climbing along the northern edge of Traprain Law, with steeper drops down to your left.

Approaching the top, the path branches again – go right for the final, steady rise onto the hill's extensive summit plateau, its top marked with a trig and a large cairn.

Traprain Law was formed around 320 million years ago by volcanic activity, with its profile then left behind after great ice sheets scoured the landscape some 14,000 years ago. By 1500BC it is thought that the hill was home to a small community; a tribe known as the Votadini occupied the site for several hundred years until the 5th century. In 1919 archaeological excavations uncovered a huge hoard of Roman silver, dating from this time. More than 250 fragments of objects that included bowls, spoons, flagons, dishes and plates, as well as more personal items such as jewellery and buckles, were discovered.

It is worth exploring the summit as the outlook is fantastic, extending towards Dunbar, North Berwick Law, Bass Rock and across the Firth of Forth to Fife. Inland, the rolling Lammermuirs crest to the south,

while looking west the familiar outline of the Pentland Hills and Arthur's Seat rear above Edinburgh's skyline. Ring ouzel, wheatear and golden plover may be seen in and around the summit during the summer with the skylark's distinctive song heard throughout the year.

From the trig marker take a clear path that bears southwest across the summit, keeping left when it splits. The path then begins to descend steadily before curving right to run northwest along Traprain Law's quieter western edge. Here you may have the best chance of spotting the Exmoor ponies, which help with grazing and conservation on the hill.

Continue along the path to the outward route and follow this back to the car park.

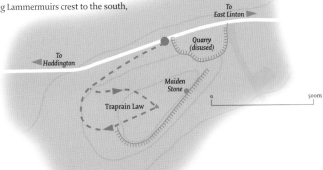

Athelstaneford and the Garleton Hills

Distance 7.25km Time 2 hours
Terrain **countryside paths and tracks,**
minor road Map **OS Explorer 351**
Access **bus from Haddington to**
Athelstaneford

If the weather is with you, this airy stroll
will give you a taste of the expansive blue
skies that are widely held to have inspired
the creation of Scotland's national flag.
The little village of Athelstaneford is where
it all started, and so too does this walk, as it
climbs into the Garleton Hills for a
sweeping overview of East Lothian.

The walk begins from the National Flag
Heritage Centre, which is housed in a
16th-century doocot in the grounds of
Athelstaneford Parish Church. The
exhibition, which is free and open from
April to October, details the history of
Scotland's national flag.

Tradition has it that in 832AD an army of
Picts and Scots, led by Angus mac Fergus,

invaded Lothian and met a Northumbrian
army led by King Athelstan, a little to the
north of where Athelstaneford stands
today. Praying for deliverance during the
tumult of battle, Angus looked skywards
to see white clouds form a cross against
the blue sky. Reminded of the martyrdom
of St Andrew, he vowed that if victorious
then St Andrew would be the Patron Saint
of Scotland. The Picts and Scots won the
day and the white and blue saltire became
the flag of Scotland.

From outside the church, cross the
B1343 and take the public path that runs
between houses, then out into open
countryside. Soon the path drops down
through two gates on either side of a
footbridge that spans the Cogtail Burn.

On the other side, turn left and pass
through another gate, then follow a field-
edge path as it veers right to climb steadily
to a track. Turn right onto this Right of Way
and continue towards the unusual ruin of

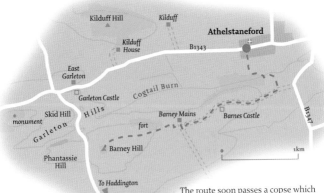

◂ Hopetoun Monument from the Garleton Hills

Barnes Castle. Known locally as 'The Vaults', work began on the castle in the late 16th century, but it was never completed as the owner, Sir John Seton of Barnes, a diplomat in the court of Philip II of Spain and later James VI's Treasurer and Lord of Session, died in 1594. Sir John also built Garleton Castle to the north of the ridge.

Just before Barney Mains Farm the track splits. Keep left and head down to a minor road, turning right to follow the well-waymarked route around the farm. After passing a row of cottages, go left onto a path that skirts the edge of a field before walking down steps to meet a track. Turn left and follow this uphill, with views to the Lammermuir Hills.

The route soon passes a copse which conceals the earthwork ramparts of a substantial hillfort. After passing through a gate, the track leads across a field to reach the high point of the walk, about 170m above sea level, beside several radio masts.

To the west is the Hopetoun Monument – also known locally as the Garleton or Galla Monument – erected in 1824 in memory of John Hope, 4th Earl of Hopetoun, while beyond lies Edinburgh, Arthur's Seat and the Pentland Hills. Traprain Law and Dunbar are also visible.

It is possible to continue in order to follow the road back to Athelstaneford; however, the traffic can be fast and it's not recommended. It is better to retrace your steps past the farm and castle, enjoying the view of the East Lothian coastline as you pick your way back to the start.

Haddington heritage loop

Distance 6.5km **Time** 2 hours
Terrain pavement, riverside and woodland
paths, minor road **Map** OS Explorer 351
Access buses from Edinburgh, Dunbar and
Berwick-upon-Tweed to Haddington

The River Tyne weaves through the heart
of this walk around the Royal Burgh of
Haddington as it does the history of the
resilient market town which, when it was
not being burned down, was subject to
several catastrophic floods. Among the
town's historic sites are one of Scotland's
oldest bridges and a collegiate church
roughed up by Henry VIII's army.
Haddington was also the birthplace of fire
and brimstone preacher John Knox.

Haddington grew as a market town from
the 12th century – at one time it was said
to be the fourth-biggest city in Scotland –
with much of its business centred around
the Mercat Cross. Over subsequent
centuries Haddington suffered a few

setbacks; the River Tyne flooded several
times and the town has been burned down
on three occasions by English armies on
their way to Edinburgh.

Haddington has a number of historically
interesting places to visit. St Mary's
Collegiate Church dates from the 1300s and,
at nearly 63m from east to west, is the
longest church in the country; the
handsome 18th-century Town House was
designed by William Adam; and the
Nungate Bridge is one of the oldest bridges
in Scotland and once served as a town
gallows. Famous people born in
Haddington include King Alexander II and
the Protestant reformer John Knox.

From the Town House on Market Street,
follow the pavement east. At Hardgate go
onto Victoria Terrace to cross Victoria
Bridge; Whittingame Drive then sweeps
you away from town. Beyond a cemetery,
turn left onto a path to cross parkland.

At the far end, go over a footbridge and

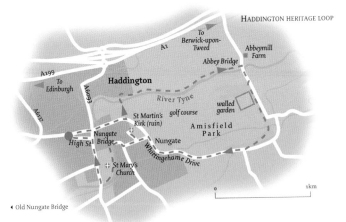

◄ Old Nungate Bridge

turn right onto Riverside Drive, then right again onto Riverside Place before joining a waterside path. Shadow this very peaceful stretch of river with views to Traprain Law.

On the far side of the River Tyne is the landscaped Amisfield Park (also home to Haddington Golf Club), created in the early 18th century with the Palladian Amisfield House as its centrepiece. The house is long gone, but the remains of the Summer House can be seen from the path.

At the three-arched Abbey Bridge, cross back over the Tyne. Follow the roadside verge, turning right into Amisfield Park when you reach the walled garden. Dating from the 18th century, it is one of Scotland's largest walled gardens.

A track skirts along the garden wall; at its far corner bear left onto a path skimming the wooded edge of the estate to eventually arrive at a gate. Turn right out of Amisfield Park here and follow a roadside path back into Haddington. Carry on along Whittingehame Drive to join Lennox Road.

A detour off Lennox Road onto Bullet Loan takes you to the enigmatic ruin of St Martin's Kirk which dates from the 12th century. In his boyhood, John Knox may have attended services here, but that did not stop the kirk falling victim to the Protestant Reformation of which he was architect.

Carry on to Bridge Street (right) to cross the river by the sandstone Nungate Bridge. As well as linking Haddington and the old village of Nungate (where John Knox lived), the bridge was on the main route to Edinburgh from the south, making it particularly vulnerable to invading armies.

Once over the bridge, turn left to pass St Mary's Collegiate Church – left roofless after the 1548 Siege of Haddington, part of Henry VIII's 'Rough Wooing' of Scotland when he tried to force an alliance through the marriage of his son and heir to the infant Mary, Queen of Scots – and continue to the B6368. Turn right for Haddington town centre, then go left onto the High Street to return to the start.

Gifford to Bolton

Distance 8km **Time** 2 hours 30 (round trip)
Terrain woodland and countryside paths,
tracks and pavement **Map** OS Explorer 351
Access buses from Haddington to Gifford

This easy route links two literary greats –
from a village whose name harks back to a
legendary sorcerer immortalised in
Sir Walter Scott's *Marmion* to the tiny
hamlet where Robert Burns' mother, sister
and brother lie buried. Paths and tracks
wend through enchanting woods and
open country, returning the same way.

The start point is Gifford, an attractive
village just over 7km south of
Haddington. Its name originates from
Hugo de Giffard, a Norman given land in
the reign of King David I, who built Yester
Castle to the south of the village in 1267.
All that remains of the once strategically
important castle is the crumbling stone
keep with atmospheric underground
vault known as Goblin Ha' which featured
in Sir Walter Scott's *Marmion*. Scott
embellished the local legend that Hugo
de Giffard was a sorcerer and warlock –
The Wizard of Yester – who had a magical
army of hobgoblins at his command.
Present-day Gifford grew up around the
gates of Yester House, built by Hugo's
descendants to replace the 'wizard's lair'.

From Gifford village centre, follow the
Haddington road north until you reach a
gate on the left signposted for Bolton.
Beyond this, a firm field-edge track skirts
woodland, soon running parallel with the
fast-flowing Colstoun Water. It then enters
a beech woodland and continues
northwest to a gate. Once through, the
walk exits the woodland and slips through
a little meadow and then alongside a field.

Beyond a gate, continue through more
enchanting woods to reach a fork. Keep
right for Bolton and, after another gate, a

◄ Bolton countryside

path rises gently away from the Colstoun Water, climbing to another gate and ploughing through scenic countryside on a track waymarked for Bolton.

The path skirts along the edge of fields where you may spot buzzard and kestrel hovering overhead. Drop gently back into a pocket of woodland before emerging into a more open landscape for a brief first glimpse of Bolton Church's steeple. Common spotted orchid and wild poppies may line the path in summer.

In a while the path widens to a track and the views extend towards Bolton and beyond, across beautiful open terrain to the Pentland Hills. Follow the track,

eventually crossing a bridge over the Gifford Water onto a rough road that climbs to gain the B6368. Turn left and follow the pavement into Bolton, which is home to Bolton Parish Church and an 18th-century doocot.

The present-day building dates from 1809, but there has been a church here since 1244. Within the kirkyard is a gravestone that was erected by Gilbert Burns, the younger brother of Robert Burns. Gilbert moved here in 1800 with his family to become a factor on a local estate and regularly attended church at Bolton where he became an elder. The grave holds the remains of Gilbert, five of his eleven children, his mother Agnes and sister Anabella. From the church turn right onto the B6368 and retrace your steps to Gifford.

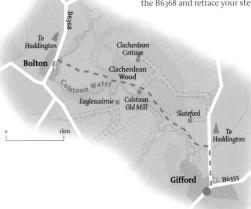

Whiteadder and Priestlaw Hill

Distance 10.5km **Time** 3 hours
Terrain hill paths and tracks, minor roads
Map OS Explorer 345 **Access** no public
transport to the start

**Explore the quiet Lammermuir Hills
south of Whiteadder Reservoir and follow
a section of the old Herring Road once
used by fishwives carrying their creels
from Dunbar to market in Lauder.**

The route begins from a small lay-by
near the northwestern edge of Whiteadder
Reservoir, beside a cattle grid on the
B6355, 13km southeast of Gifford. Follow
the access road for Priestlaw Farm along
the western fringe of Whiteadder
Reservoir, which was constructed in the
late 1960s to supply water to the towns of
East Lothian and Cockenzie Power
Station. Birdlife out on the water includes
pochard, shelduck, great-crested grebes
and wintering flocks of barnacle and
pink-footed geese.

After 650m turn right onto a track
for the 'Herring Road to Lauder' and
continue as it rises gently towards
Penshiel. Just before the farm, turn left
through a gate and follow the track as it
tramps south across a windswept portion
of moorland. This is a section of the
historic Herring Road that ran for 45km
between Dunbar and Lauder in the
Scottish Borders. Its heyday was during
the 18th and 19th centuries when
fishwives carried huge creels of herring
from Dunbar to the markets in Lauder
before returning with reserves of salted
herring for winter.

Follow the route between the two ruins
of Grange, enjoying a wonderful view of
Whiteadder Reservoir and Spartleton.
The moorland is home to lapwing, grouse,
kestrel and even hen harrier. After nearly
3km of easy walking the track drops down
to cross a bridge over the fast-flowing
Faseny Water, then goes through two

◄ Across Whiteadder Reservoir to Spartleton

gates before arriving at a minor road.

Keep left and follow this quiet road (keeping an eye out for traffic) on a steady climb for 2km to a track on the left signed for Garvald and Whiteadder Reservoir. Follow this north towards Priestlaw Hill, with views on a clear day opening out as far as the Cheviot Hills.

The track soon begins to descend gently as it veers northeast around the eastern slopes of Priestlaw Hill but, just as it curves right, look out for a grassy track on the left. This rises steadily towards the summit, splitting on the approach. Keep left for the 428m top, marked with a cairn.

After taking in the views across the Scottish Borders, return to the main track and continue. The gradual descent is accompanied by

stunning views over Whiteadder Reservoir to Spartleton and Bothwell Hill – in winter the honking of geese will be unmistakable. A steeper drop takes you to a gate just south of the reservoir and a track which leads through the farm and houses of Priestlaw. Cross the Faseny Water to meet the outward route and return to the start.

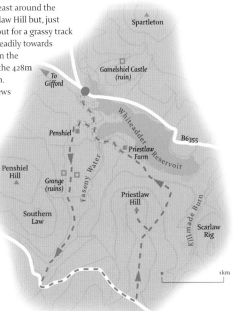

Gamelshiel Castle and Spartleton

Distance 7.25km Time 2 hours 30
Terrain hill paths and tracks
Map OS Explorer 345 Access no public
transport to the start

Climb from Whiteadder Reservoir to the crumbling remains of Gamelshiel Castle and on to Spartleton, the windswept high point of the moorland on the edge of Dunbar Common.

Start from a small parking area on the north side of the B6355 above Whiteadder Reservoir, 13km southeast of Gifford. Go through a gate and follow a track northwest alongside the Whiteadder Water, home to wintering pink-footed geese and scaup.

After 400m the track splits; keep right on a grassy trail which climbs steadily east, under the slopes of Summer Hill and

alongside the Hall Burn, to reach the scant remains of Gamelshiel Castle. Today only two walls, which are around 1m thick, remain of this towerhouse which is thought to date from the 16th century. Surrounded on three sides by moorland and hidden from any road it is a secluded and atmospheric spot.

A few feet beyond the castle, a narrow path peels left from the track and easily crosses the Hall Burn, after which it climbs steadily up the lower western slopes of Spartleton. The moorland landscape is home to kestrel, lapwing, grey wagtail and snipe while views open out towards a number of the Lammermuir Hills, including

Priestlaw Hill, Kingside Hill and Bleak Law.

In a while the path widens to a grassy track, then after a short descent it climbs steadily again all the way to a fence. Follow the track to reach a gap in the fence and turn right through it. Here, a vague path climbs to a track. Keep right and follow it all the way to the top of Spartleton. A large windfarm sits below to the north, but a fine panorama extends across Dunbar Common and the rolling Lammermuirs and east to the Berwickshire coast.

Return through the gap in the fence, then immediately turn right and follow a grassy track alongside the fence. The ground here is generally featureless and, in poor visibility, close attention needs to be paid to the track and fence. Continue on a gentle descent for 1km to pass under the line of electricity pylons that sit on Ling Rig and reach a junction.

Turn right for 50m, go left onto another track, then after a few steps keep left onto the waymarked Herring Road. This was used during the 18th and 19th centuries by fishwives who transported their creels

of herring from Dunbar to the markets at Lauder. A stony track follows the line of this historic route as it sweeps left and gradually descends, with good views of Priestlaw Hill and Penshiel Hill. Continue all the way down to the Whiteadder Water.

Just before a gate, go left and follow a grassy track alongside the eastern bank of the river, soon returning to the outward route at the base of Summer Hill. Retrace your steps to the start.

◀ Gamelshiel Castle

Pressmennan Wood

**Distance 4.75km Time 1 hour 30
Terrain woodland paths and tracks
Map OS Explorer 351 Access no public
transport to the start; buses from Dunbar
to Stenton, leaving 2.5km to the start**

**Weave through a fragment of Scotland's
ancient oakwoods by the shores of
Pressmennan Lake, then make your way
along a fun sculpture trail on a route
that's ideal for families and young
children with plenty of wildlife, both real
and represented, to seek out.**

Pressmennan Wood sits 2.5km south of
the village of Stenton. There is no public
transport direct to the start, but there is a
small car park at the entrance to the wood.

From the car park walk a few metres back
along the access road, then turn right at a
yellow marker boulder. Descend a path to
a track, turning right, then immediately

right again onto a trail that threads its way
northeast through a fragment of
Scotland's ancient oakwoods, where there
are also stands of mature ash and hazel.

Today this site is managed by the
Woodland Trust Scotland who, over the
next 100 years, will plant more native
species such as oak, birch, ash and rowan
instead of the mixture of conifer species,
such as Norway spruce, Douglas fir and
larch, planted by the Forestry Commission
during the 1950s. This woodland is
believed to have produced quality oak
timber in the past.

Very soon the path runs alongside lovely
Pressmennan Lake where a bench is a good
vantage point for spotting wildlife – you
have a chance of spying roe deer,
woodpecker and even otter. The path then
undulates gently above the lake. Beyond
the Wavey Wood Post, keep your eyes at

ground level for a pair of doorways hidden at the bases of two inconspicuous trees. Be very quiet as this is where Odon Poolittle and Bombi Noffnuff live. The path then curves right and eventually emerges at a T-junction beside a wooden carving known as the Holey Posty.

Turn left, leaving the sculpture trail for now, and follow a track high above the lake before taking an indistinct path on the left which drops quite steeply down to the water – the path becomes clearer as it descends, but can also be a bit muddy. Bound by picturesque woodland, the lakeside is home to bats and owls, with primrose, bluebell and wood sorrel among the wildflowers it is noted for.

A paved path with a railing runs beside the lake. Just before its end – if you go through a gate you have gone too far – turn right onto a faint grassy trail that plunges back into the woods. It becomes clearer before swinging right to reach the end of the track you left earlier on.

Follow the track as it rises gradually west, soon passing the path that dropped down to the lake. From here, retrace your steps to the Holey Posty. Keep straight on along the sculpture trail, passing more carvings, to return to the car park.

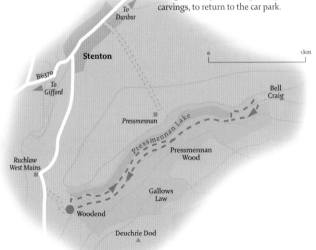

As well as the miles of stunning coastline between Musselburgh and Dunbar, East Lothian is renowned for its welcoming towns and villages, world-famous championship links golf courses, glorious golden beaches and wonderful walking routes.

Musselburgh is one of the oldest towns in Scotland, having been inhabited since Roman times, and has seen its fair share of conflict with our southern neighbours. To the east is the spectacular beach that links Gullane with Aberlady, surely one of the finest in Scotland.

The charming settlement of Dirleton is built around its village green and castle, which dates from the 13th-century. Off the coast to the north is the island of Fidra, thought to be the inspiration for Robert Louis Stevenson's *Treasure Island*.

Perhaps the best vantage point to survey all of East Lothian and beyond is North Berwick Law. Its conical outline can be seen from miles around and the view from the 187m summit extends across a good portion of southern Scotland.

Ravensheugh Sands is a hidden gem of a beach, while Dunbar is another of East Lothian's popular holiday towns with a rugged coastline that gives way to the sweeping Belhaven Bay. Its most famous son is John Muir, the celebrated conservationist, naturalist and explorer. The John Muir Country Park, on the outskirts of Dunbar, holds a variety of habitats and a huge diversity of flora and fauna; a fitting tribute to the man whose commitment to the environment led to the preservation of countless wild areas across the world.

Bass Rock from Berwick Law ▶

East Lothian coast

Musselburgh and Pinkie Cleugh

Distance 6.75km Time 2 hours
Terrain countryside and parkland paths
and tracks, pavement Map OS Explorer 351
Access trains from Edinburgh and North
Berwick to Musselburgh; buses from
Edinburgh to Musselburgh

South of Musselburgh, in the open
country between Inveresk and Wallyford,
is the site of the Battle of Pinkie Cleugh,
the biggest and bloodiest battle ever
fought in Scotland. It took place in 1547
and was the last pitched battle fought
between the separate kingdoms of
England and Scotland. This route
travels through scenic countryside to
visit its memorial.

Start from the corner of Bridge Street
and High Street in Musselburgh. The town
developed through its fishing industry,
woollen mills and coal mining while the
name Musselburgh stems from the mussel
beds that lie along the firth.

Follow the High Street east through the
town, passing the 16th-century Tolbooth
before turning right onto Newbigging,
which rises gradually to a junction with
Inveresk Road. Go right, then left, and
continue past Lewisvale Park to reach
Inveresk Village Road and pass the
entrance to Inveresk Estate. Inveresk is a
conservation village lined with picturesque
houses, the most striking being the Manor
House, which dates from 1748.

Soon the road splits, so bear left onto
Crookston Road and continue away from
Inveresk village into beautiful open
countryside. Once across a railway bridge,
an old road continues southeast – the
adjacent fields were the site of the Battle of
Pinkie Cleugh. The road soon narrows to a
paved path and veers left to run alongside
the A6094, emerging at an old section of
road. Follow this past a cottage to reach
the battle's memorial stone, which was
erected in 1998.

The battle was the culmination of many years of discord between Henry VIII and the Scottish Parliament, a period known as the 'Rough Wooing' as Henry tried to secure his northern border through the forced marriage of his son, Prince Edward, to the young Scottish Queen Mary. The conflict was arguably the first modern battle on British soil as it featured infantry, cavalry and artillery as well as naval bombardment from the English navy positioned in the Firth of Forth. Superior English forces and tactical mistakes meant that 10 September 1547 became known as 'Black Saturday'; it is thought as many as 6000 Scots were killed with around 500 losses on the English side.

Carry on to reach Salter's Road (A6094), and descend towards Wallyford before turning left onto a rough road (signposted for Pinkie and Musselburgh) and follow it

down towards a small industrial estate. Just before this, turn right onto a public path and walk to the right of the site, then bear left to duck beneath a railway bridge.

From here a path continues through lovely countryside and descends to Pinkie, a residential area just east of Musselburgh. Cross Pinkiehill Crescent onto Pinkie Drive; at a roundabout, bear right and then left onto Edenhall Crescent. After a few paces, keep right and follow a paved path over parkland to a roundabout at Edenhall Bank.

Here, a path runs between houses and crosses Lewisvale Avenue to reach the corner of Park Lane. Go straight on into the attractive surrounds of Lewisvale Park. Walk all the way through the park, exiting right onto Inveresk Brae. From here you can retrace your steps to the start.

Gullane and Aberlady Bay

Distance 9.5km **Time** 2 hours 30
Terrain coastal and countryside paths
and tracks **Map** OS Explorer 351
Access buses from Edinburgh and North
Berwick to Gullane

The section of coastline between
Gullane and Aberlady is one of the finest
in Scotland. An exquisite sandy beach
backed by wind-ruffled dunes drifts along
Gullane Bay to Gullane Point, beyond
which is Aberlady Local Nature Reserve.
A stretch of the John Muir Way returns to
Gullane to complete one of East Lothian's
best walks.

Begin by facing the ruin of St Andrews
Kirk at the west end of Gullane's Main
Street. It is thought that a church was first
established here during the 800s, although
most of what remains dates from later.

Turn left, then right onto West Links

Road and follow it to its end. Once through
a gate beside Gullane No 1 Golf Course,
bear right and climb steeply west up a
grassy hill to the corner of a wall.

Here, pick up an obvious path that rises
north, to the left of the wall, to gain the
summit of Gullane Hill. The view from the
top takes in the Pentland Hills and
Edinburgh. Continue across the summit to
pick up a track to the right of the 7th tee.

Follow this as it descends west. When it
splits, keep right and continue, enjoying
views over windswept Gullane Bents.
When the path forks again, keep left,
following the sign for Gullane Point to a
waymarked path on the right. This carries
on high above the coast, through dune
grass, towards Hummell Rocks.

At a junction turn right onto a track and,
just before a line of World War Two
concrete block defences, keep right where

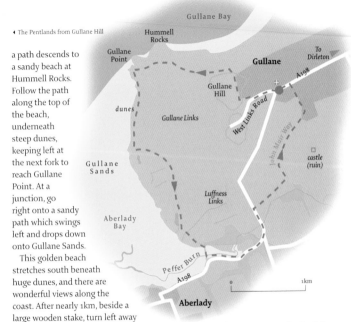

◀ The Pentlands from Gullane Hill

a path descends to a sandy beach at Hummell Rocks. Follow the path along the top of the beach, underneath steep dunes, keeping left at the next fork to reach Gullane Point. At a junction, go right onto a sandy path which swings left and drops down onto Gullane Sands.

This golden beach stretches south beneath huge dunes, and there are wonderful views along the coast. After nearly 1km, beside a large wooden stake, turn left away from the beach and climb over the dunes into Aberlady Local Nature Reserve.

During autumn, more than 30,000 pink-footed geese fly in from Iceland to feed before moving on during winter. Wheatears, whitethroat, blackcaps, redshank and lapwing may also be seen at different times of the year.

A good track heads east through the reserve. In a while turn right at a crossroads and continue south, soon passing through a pocket of woodland. You eventually leave the reserve via an old wooden bridge to emerge at the A198. For a break, Aberlady is well worth the short detour (right) from here.

To continue the walk, turn left and follow the John Muir Way beside the A198 for around 1.5km. Just before the entrance to Luffness Links Golf Club, carefully cross the road and go through a gate. Here, the John Muir Way continues towards Gullane along a field-edge path.

Nearing Gullane, pass through a gate and keep straight on to Saltcoats Road. Turn left and return along Gullane Main Street.

Dirleton, Yellowcraig and Fidra

Distance 5.25km **Time** 1 hour 30
Terrain countryside and coastal paths and
tracks, minor road **Map** OS Explorer 351
Access buses from Edinburgh and North
Berwick to Dirleton

**Thought to have been the inspiration for
Robert Louis Stevenson's *Treasure Island*,
the little isle of Fidra sits just off the coast
at Yellowcraig, a short distance from the
pretty village of Dirleton. This easy walk
follows countryside paths and a minor
road to reach Broad Sands Bay where there
are fine views of Fidra and much of the
East Lothian coast.**

Begin the walk from Dirleton Castle on
the main road through the village. The
castle was built during the 13th century
and its fortified walls were home to the de
Vaux, Haliburton and Ruthven families for
the next 400 years until Oliver Cromwell
and his army laid siege to it in 1650. The
Nisbet family then transformed the castle

remains into a designed landscape in the
1660s, while the gardens today date from
the late 19th and early 20th centuries.
Dirleton Castle is cared for by Historic
Environment Scotland and is open daily.

From the castle, follow Manse Road to
the left of the green, away from the village
centre. When the road splits, keep right
and continue past several houses along a
section of the John Muir Way – a little to
the left stands the 17th-century Dirleton
Parish Church.

Carry on along the track when the road
ends and, once across the bridge over the
slender Eel Burn, go right (leaving the John
Muir Way) to continue east towards
Dirleton New Mains Farm. Go through the
farm and past a few houses to reach Ware
Road. Keep left and follow the narrow road,
which is the main access for the car park at
Yellowcraig; be wary of traffic. After nearly
1km the road ends at the car park. Here
keep straight on, go through a gate and

take a track, then a sandy path to reach the western edge of Broad Sands Bay.

Fidra sits out in the Firth of Forth and forms part of the Forth Islands Special Protection Area, which also includes the neighbouring islands of Craigleith and Lamb. Fidra is an important breeding ground for puffins, guillemots, shags and razorbills.

Robert Louis Stevenson visited Yellowcraig many times – Fidra Lighthouse was built by his father Thomas and cousin David – and it is thought that the map of *Treasure Island* was based on Fidra. The ruins of St Nicholas's Priory, dating from 1165, can also still be seen on the island. The chapel was used as a *lazaretto*, or hospital for those with infectious diseases, and passing ships landed sick crew members on Fidra to be quarantined until they were well enough to enter port further up the Firth. Today the uninhabited island is an RSPB Scotland nature reserve, and remotely operated cameras send live pictures of the birdlife back to watching visitors at the

Scottish Seabird Centre in North Berwick.

Retrace your steps towards Yellowcraig car park but, just before the entrance gate, turn right for Dirleton where the John Muir Way makes its way through the woodland of Yellow Craig Plantation. It soon veers left away from the woods onto a wide track that heads south across a field with lovely views of Dirleton and the distant cone of North Berwick Law.

The track continues all the way back to the bridge over the Eel Burn and the outward route down Manse Road.

◄ Fidra from Yellowcraig

North Berwick Law

Distance 4km **Time** 1 hour 30
Terrain hill paths, pavement; steep ascent
and descent **Map** OS Explorer 351
Access no public transport to the start;
trains and buses from Edinburgh to North
Berwick, leaving around 1km to the start

Formed by volcanic activity around 300
million years ago, North Berwick Law only
rises to 187m above the East Lothian
coastline, but it has a giant presence in
the landscape. The climb is steep and the
path a little exposed when nearing the
top, but the route is straightforward. You
may also spot a small semi-feral herd of
Exmoor ponies on the way up.

The walk begins from The Law Car Park,
which is just off Haddington Road (B1347)
on the outskirts of North Berwick. Cross
the stone stile at the back of the car park,
go through a gate and bear right onto the
John Muir Way. Here, a track contours
south around the base of North Berwick

Law, its steep slopes rising to the left. After
a short distance, leave the John Muir Way
by turning left onto a path signposted for
the summit.

A steep climb brings you quickly to a
bench. Take another path on the left here
which rises steeply through craggy
outcrops to a flatter section. Keep left onto
a wider path and walk to a second bench,
where coastal views open out. The route
now curves right. There are a variety of
paths, but the most scenic keeps to the
northern edge of North Berwick Law and,
although a little exposed, with steep
slopes dropping to the left, the steady rise
soon gains the summit trig pillar and
replica pair of whale jawbones sited within
a small enclosure.

The first whalebones were placed here in
1709 as a beacon for sailors, but were
blown down in a gale in 1935. A second set
only lasted until 2005, and the current pair
(made of fibreglass this time) were

◄ Whalebone arch on
North Berwick Law

installed in
2008. Just
beneath the top
is a small ruin
that was used as a
signal station and lookout
post during the Napoleonic
Wars and World War Two. The view is
spectacular, taking in the East Lothian and
Fife coastlines, Edinburgh, Arthur's Seat,
the Pentland and Ochil Hills, and the big
mountains of the Southern Highlands.

Carefully retrace your steps to the flatter
area above the lower bench. Turn left here
onto a path that skirts eastwards around
North Berwick Law's southern edge to
reach a junction. Go right, following a path
through a line of hawthorn and gorse
bushes to a gate.

Once through this, continue along a
field-edge path to shortly pass through
another gate, where you turn left onto a
track. This leads to a minor road at Heugh

Steadings; keep right when it splits and
descend to Heugh Brae (look out for a
particularly fine old doocot in a field to the
right). Turn left and follow the pavement,
which ends when Heugh Brae sweeps left.
Carefully follow the roadside verge back
into North Berwick where a pavement
continues to a roundabout.

Keep left onto Dunbar Road (A198),
then left at Lochbridge Road. Follow this
to Law View, turn left and go down a
gravel path to a T-junction. Turn right
and walk along another path that rises
gradually to the car park access road
beside the B1347. Turn left and go along
a path to reach the start.

89

Ravensheugh Sands

Distance 5km **Time** 2 hours
Terrain woodland paths and tracks, beach; at very high tides the beach may be impassable **Map** OS Explorer 351 **Access** no public transport to the start; bus from North Berwick and Dunbar to Limetree Walk road end, leaving 2km to the start

As beaches go, Ravensheugh Sands is close to perfect. There is no car park, caravan park or ice-cream van here, so it has a secluded feel, offers great views towards Bass Rock and is an excellent place to spot coastal birdlife. The woodland paths, wildlife-rich dunes and sandy beach make this simple walk a real delight.

Walk east through Tyninghame Links car park, which sits at the eastern end of Limetree Walk. Nearby is the early 19th-century red sandstone Tyninghame House, residence of the Earls of Haddington. The 6th Earl, Thomas Hamilton, was a pioneer of agricultural improvement and planted tens of thousands of trees on his estate, as well as designing the avenues and walled garden. He also wrote several important pamphlets, including *A Treatise on the Manner of Raising Forest Trees*, which was published in 1761.

Join a track and follow it as it curves right to reach two gates. Take the left one and continue southeast along a lovely woodland track, where views extend across the fields of rural East Lothian. Stick to the main track to arrive at the shoreline beside the outflow of the River Tyne. Redshank, teal, oystercatcher, greenshank, and golden and ringed plover are among the selection of birdlife that may be spotted here through the seasons.

Keep left on a woodland path as it dodges its way through a line of large concrete blocks, anti-tank traps that date from World War Two. Go right at the next junction onto a track and follow this out of the woodland onto coastal grassland. Ahead is the rocky shelf of St Baldred's Cradle and a large red sandstone seat.

St Baldred, 'the Apostle of the Lothians', is thought to have arrived here from Northumberland, via Ireland, some time during the 8th century. He established a monastery and then a chapel on Bass Rock where he undertook a number of retreats and is thought to have died in 757.

If the tide is high then the beach may be impassable and so you need to retrace your steps to the start. If the tide is low then bear northwest from the seat along a grassy and then sandy path before descending onto Ravensheugh Sands. Walk along the beach, beneath towering dunes and enjoy expansive views along the coast. Just after a wooden post, as the dunes shrink in size, bear left from the beach onto a sandy path that crosses over them. Go through two gates to reach a track.

Follow the sign for Tyninghame Links car park southeast alongside the dunes. The track soon sweeps right and rises gently back into the woodland of Tyninghame Links. When it splits keep left and continue, eventually passing through a final gate after which a right turn leads back to the start.

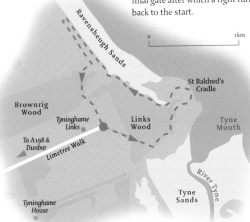

John Muir Country Park

Distance 3.5km **Time** 1 hour
Terrain woodland and coastal paths
Map OS Explorer 351 **Access** no public
transport to the start; buses from
Edinburgh to West Barns, leaving just
under 1km to the start

John Muir Country Park sits on the
outskirts of Dunbar and is named after
the conservationist, naturalist and
explorer John Muir, who was born in
the town in 1838. The park, which
takes in the wonderful stretch of East
Lothian coastline between Belhaven
Bay and Tyninghame, is home to a
variety of habitats, including estuary,
dunes and woodland, making it a
haven for wildlife.

The walk begins from Linkfield Car Park,
which sits 750m north of Edinburgh Road
(A1087) at West Barns. Pick up the John
Muir Way at the southeastern corner of the

car park and turn left. Here a path makes
its way to the right of Hedderwick Hill
Plantation, passing the car park and then
public toilets. A few metres after
this, keep left at a fork and follow the John
Muir Way west along the southern edge
of the woodland.

The path, which provides easy, enjoyable
walking, takes you past a farm park with
fine views inland across East Lothian's
great tracts of agricultural land to the
northern edge of the rolling Lammermuir
Hills. There are a number of paths, but
keep to the John Muir Way as it runs along
the edge of the predominantly Scots pine
woodland, keeping an eye out for grey
squirrel and green woodpecker.

After 1km the John Muir Way reaches the
Tyne Estuary, where the River Tyne enters
the North Sea. There are lovely views
across the estuary to Sandy Hirst and Tyne
Sands, but it is the huge range of birdlife

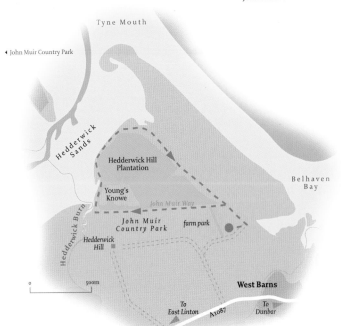

that impresses; curlew, oystercatcher, turnstone, shelduck, brent goose, cormorant, wigeon, sparrowhawk, mute swan, goldeneye, teal, gadwall, great black-backed gull, purple sandpiper, sanderling, greenshank, redshank, dunlin, bar-tailed godwit and golden and ringed plover might be spotted during the seasons.

From here, take a path on the right, leaving the John Muir Way behind, and head northeast along the northern edge of the woodland. When the path splits, keep left and continue alongside the estuary.

In a while the path exits the woodland as it swings right and carries on southeast through marram grass, where cinnabar moth, small copper butterfly, skylark and meadow pipit may well be spied. Continue through the grassland where the walking is delightful and views extend towards the jagged coastline just west of Dunbar.

Eventually you come to a bridge to cross a boggy section of ground, after which the outward path is regained at the corner of Hedderwick Hill Plantation. Keep straight on along the John Muir Way and return to the car park.

Dunbar and Belhaven Bay

Distance 6.25km **Time** 2 hours
Terrain pavement, coastal paths
Map OS Explorer 351 **Access** trains from
Edinburgh to Dunbar; buses from
Edinburgh and Berwick-upon-Tweed
to Dunbar

Dunbar prospered in the 18th century
as one of Scotland's major herring ports
and it is still a bustling town with a
working harbour. It is also the birthplace
of John Muir – naturalist, explorer,
environmental philosopher and early
advocate for the preservation of
wilderness. This walk follows some of
the John Muir Way, a 215km cross-country
route named in his honour.

From Dunbar Railway Station, walk
along Station Road, turn left onto
Countess Road, then right onto Abbey
Road and follow this to the High Street.
Keep left through the town, passing a fine

statue of a young John Muir and the
excellent John Muir Birthplace Museum.

Muir spent much of his childhood
exploring the shoreline of Dunbar and
wandering in the local countryside, before
emigrating to America with his family
just before his 11th birthday in 1849. His
early enthusiasm for the natural world led
him to study botany at university, but it
was a workplace accident in a wagon
wheel factory which led him to 'follow his
dream of exploration and study of plants'.

He walked from Kentucky to Florida
before settling in San Francisco and
campaigning for the preservation of
Yosemite valley in California, which was
declared a National Park in 1890. In 1892
he co-founded the Sierra Club which
became one of the world's most
important environmental organisations,
and his many essays and widely-read
books inspired presidents and

congressmen to take action to preserve the American wilderness.

At a roundabout, opposite the striking 18th-century Lauderdale House, turn right and go down Victoria Street to reach Victoria Harbour, which dates from 1842.

Bear left just after the RNLI Lifeboat Station to join the John Muir Way and follow this along the quayside. Above stands the thin wedge of Dunbar Castle, which is thought to have been built in the 12th century – although a defensive site probably existed on this clifftop location from Roman times. Dunbar translates from Cumbric as 'Fort on the Height'.

At the end of the harbour go left onto Castle Gate, then right onto a paved path that passes along the front of Dunbar Leisure Centre. Go straight through the

car park and down a flight of steps to follow the John Muir Way as it skirts along East Lothian's rocky coast. The route continues high above the coast on a paved esplanade with far-reaching views of Bass Rock, Traprain Law, North Berwick Law and Belhaven Bay's arc of golden sand.

At the end of the esplanade walk down some steps and carry on along the edge of the golf course, eventually reaching the eastern edge of dune-backed Belhaven Bay. You can carry on and explore the beach and dunes, all part of the John Muir Country Park, or return to the start by following Back Road along the edge of the golf course to the town centre.

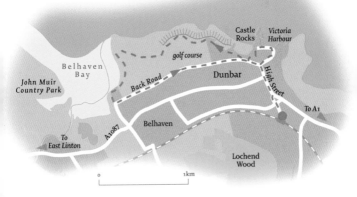

◂ Coastline at Dunbar

Index